ECONOMICS TAKES A HOLIDAY

Celebrations from the Dismal Science

By

HOLLEY HEWITT ULBRICH

abbott press®
A DIVISION OF WRITER'S DIGEST

ECONOMICS TAKES A HOLIDAY
CELEBRATIONS FROM THE DISMAL SCIENCE

Copyright © 2013 Holley Hewitt Ulbrich.

All rights reserved. No part of this book may be used or reproduced by any means, graphic, electronic, or mechanical, including photocopying, recording, taping or by any information storage retrieval system without the written permission of the publisher except in the case of brief quotations embodied in critical articles and reviews.

Abbott Press books may be ordered through booksellers or by contacting:

Abbott Press
1663 Liberty Drive
Bloomington, IN 47403
www.abbottpress.com
Phone: 1-866-697-5310

Because of the dynamic nature of the Internet, any web addresses or links contained in this book may have changed since publication and may no longer be valid. The views expressed in this work are solely those of the author and do not necessarily reflect the views of the publisher, and the publisher hereby disclaims any responsibility for them.

Any people depicted in stock imagery provided by Thinkstock are models, and such images are being used for illustrative purposes only.

Certain stock imagery © Thinkstock.

ISBN: 978-1-4582-0761-6 (sc)
ISBN: 978-1-4582-0763-0 (e)
ISBN: 978-1-4582-0762-3 (hc)

Library of Congress Control Number: 2012923863

Printed in the United States of America

Abbott Press rev. date: 01/07/2013

CONTENTS

1. January 1

    1st—New Year's Day: Credible Commitment 1

    15th—Martin Luther King Jr.: Prophet of
        Nonviolence 5

2. February 11

    2nd—Ground Hog Day: Punxatawney Phil and
        Economic Forecasting 11

    14th—Valentine's Day: Heartless Capitalism? 15

    3rd Monday—President's Day: What Makes a
        Leader? 19

3. March 23

    17th—St. Patrick's Day: Snakes and Ants 23

    20th/21st—Vernal Equinox: Our Fancy Turns to
        Better Mousetraps 27

4. April 31

    15th—Income Tax Day: Flat and Simple, or Fair and
        Complicated? 31

    22nd—Earth Day: Property Rights 35

5. May 39
- 1ˢᵗ—May Day: Fertility and Population 39
- 2ⁿᵈ Sunday—Mother's Day: All Mothers are Working Mothers 44

6. June 47
- 14ᵗʰ—Flag Day: How Big Should a Country Be? 47
- 3ʳᵈ Sunday—Fathers' Day: The Changing American Family 52

7. July 57
- July—The Month of Revolutions 57
- 14ᵗʰ—Bastille Day: The Costs of Inequality 61

8. August 65
- August—The Month with No Holidays 65

9. September 71
- 1ˢᵗ Monday—Labor Day: Minimum Wage, Living Wage 71
- 1ˢᵗ Sunday after Labor Day—Grandparent's Day: Paying for the Golden Years 76
- 20ᵗʰ/21ˢᵗ—The Autumn Equinox: Turning Points and the Business Cycle 80

10. October 85
- 12ᵗʰ—Columbus Day: The First Wave of Immigration 85
- 21ˢᵗ—Alfred Nobel's Birthday: The Nobel Prize in Economics 89

    31st—Halloween: Taking Chances..............................94

11. November 97

    11th—Veterans' Day: Paying What We Owe 97

    4th Thursday—Thanksgiving: Affirming Our
        Values 101

12. December 105

    5th—National Volunteer Day: Working for
        Nothing 105

    6th—Saint Nicholas Day: Is There a Santa Claus?... 110

    Late December—Winter Solstice/Christmas/
        Hanukkah: Throwing Hope into the
        Darkness 113

    26th—Boxing Day: Opening the Box 117

ECONOMICS TAKES A HOLIDAY

It began as an innocent love affair between an economist and the calendar. Named (unintentionally) after Mother Holle, an ancient Celtic goddess of the underworld who gave good things to good people and left coal for the bad ones, I was destined to have a fascination with holidays. As a child, I loved Christmas, 4th of July, first day of school, Valentine's Day, Halloween, New Year's Day, and Thanksgiving. And as I grew up, earned college degrees and became an economist, and married and had children, I continued to discover appealing holidays, including some fairly obscure ones like Imbolc, a Celtic purification festival held on the first of February in anticipation of spring. But it wasn't until the early 1970s that I connected holidays to my profession of economics.

It was 1973, and Russell Shannon, my friend and colleague in the Clemson University Department of Economics, was coordinating a series of weekly columns in a regional newspaper. One day, I told him I wanted to write a column for Valentine's Day and call it "Heartless Capitalism." When he asked what it was about, I said, "I don't know, I only have a title." It wasn't a particular topic that had captivated my attention, but rather the idea of linking economics with holidays.

And so my Holley-days, as Russell called them, were launched. He suggested that they be collected in a book, but they never were. By the time I considered the idea again, more than three decades had elapsed, and I was a different kind of economist. Neo-institutional and behavioral economics had begun to take hold in certain parts of the profession, challenging many of the conclusions that traditional (or neoclassical, as they are known) economists drew from their abstract models and statistical analyses. This shift suited me. It addressed some of the limitations of the abstract by grounding the field more in the real world. It also made me rethink the power of holidays as a tool for exploring human behavior.

Neoclassical economics relies heavily on a rather simple but quite serviceable model of human behavior: the rational, self-interested individual who uses his resources and skills to maximize his personal well-being and in the process (but as an incidental byproduct of self-interest) benefits society as a whole. This rational, economic man is a calculating machine with perfect information and tastes and preferences that are impervious to change. Furthermore, the principles of neoclassical economics are timeless and universal. They should apply as well to choices in an Inuit village or a Chinese megalopolis as they do to the Western culture in which they were developed. The laws of traditional economics mimic the laws of physics as natural and immutable.

Behavioral economics, drawing heavily on psychology, suggests that human motivation is more complex than simple self-interest. Preferences or tastes are not fixed; they change with a person's experience, with advertising, and with the opinions of friends and family. It turns out that humans are not such simple calculating machines as the model of rational, economic man might suggest.

Our motives include concern for the well-being of others as well as ourselves. Our search for meaning is at least as deep as our search for comfort, security, and other economic goods. Our preferences are not entirely inborn—infants are not born with a craving for Big Macs—but influenced to a large degree by our cultures. Our processes of gathering and digesting information are subject to our limits of time and mental capability. In practice, we operate with less than perfect information and rely on rules of thumb in many of our market choices.

Neo-institutional economics reminds us that we and the economies/societies in which we live exist in a historical and cultural context, not in a vacuum. That context limits the range of options we consider and influences both our preferences and our choices. One of the insights of neo-institutional economics is the path-dependent state. In simple English, a path-dependent state means that we are where we are largely because we have been where we have been, and that limits the options we have at this choice point.

Both behavioral and neo-institutional changes to the dominant economic model suggest that choices and outcomes are, in many cases, likely to be quite different from what the traditional model would predict.

What does this have to do with holidays? Rather than being about the individual in the abstract, holidays are about communities, cultures, history, and our relationship with the natural world. Both altruism—concern for the well-being of others—and cultural and historical influences on tastes and preferences come to the fore when we look at the rational, calculating self-interested individual in a context of community, history, and the natural world. Holidays offer a way to highlight that context--the history, culture and geography within which we make our choices. And since holidays are scattered throughout the year, this book offers a chance to explore some of the emerging ideas of behavioral and neo-institutional economics in small, seasonal doses.

So put on your party hat and allow me to introduce you to the new world of behavioral, contextual, interpersonal, historical economics, one holiday at a time.

 # JANUARY

1ST—NEW YEAR'S DAY: CREDIBLE COMMITMENT

The first of January, the start of the new year, is a time of new beginnings. It embodies many traditions of starting over. Partying the night before is about ringing out the old, ringing in the new. In the South, the traditional midday meal of collard greens, black-eyed peas, and fatback is supposed to attract good luck and prosperity for the coming year. Year-end articles recap the best photos, greatest sports moments, celebrity deaths, a kind of closure before moving on to the next twelve months. And then, there are New Year's resolutions. People commit themselves to quitting smoking, losing weight, exercising more, watching television less, spending more time with family, being more frugal, and a variety of other intended improvements in their personal, work, or family and community life.

Economists refer to these commitments to resist temptations

as meta-preferences—preferences about preferences. I may prefer French fries to apples, but I also prefer thinner to fatter. At least on New Year's Day, and for as long as possible thereafter, I want to commit to thinner over fatter and thus apples over French fries. I may have to find ways to bind myself to that commitment, much as Ulysses bound himself (literally, to the mast) to resist the call of the sirens in the *Odyssey*. There are a variety of steps I can take to increase the odds of honoring that commitment. I can join weight watchers. I can diet with a friend. I can keep a food journal in which I have to confess every fall from dietary grace. I can publicly proclaim my goal. All of these devices will increase the likelihood that I will keep my commitment.

Commitment to change, or to staying the course, is not just a personal issue. While we may not expect to keep our New Year's resolutions, we do expect our governments' commitments to be credible. Changes in government policies affect our individual decisions. Tax breaks for fuel efficient cars and better home insulation alter our choices. The Affordable Care Act will certainly change a lot of choices by individuals and firms. Cap and trade on emissions, credit card regulations, bank bailouts, changes in the estate tax—all of these policies affect people's decisions about work, career choices, risk-taking, borrowing, investing, and lending.

But governments themselves change. Elections often change the party in power, and policy changes come with that shift. While some of our personal decisions are pretty short term, others—choosing a career, buying a house, investing for retirement—are long-term. We need to have some idea of whether a policy change is temporary or permanent, or at least reasonably long term. Nowhere was that demand for a credible commitment by government more evident than in the debate over privatizing Social Security. Individuals who had made life plans that included Social Security as currently structured would be affected adversely by a shift to an individual retirement plan, especially those close to retirement.

How can governments make credible commitments when those in power serve two, four, or six-year terms? How can they bind future governments to honoring their commitments? Certainly citizen pressure does the trick on certain issues, like Social Security. Putting policies in the constitution are another way to make credible commitments, because it is typically more difficult to change a constitution than to rewrite a law.

There is, however, a downside risk to making too many commitments, especially those that involve money. Governments need both stability and flexibility. If all their commitments are written in stone, they have few choices or options when fiscal circumstances change. State governments discovered and rediscovered that challenge in the fiscal crisis of 2001-03 and again in the financial crisis starting in 2008. Unlike the federal government, all but one of the fifty states are required to balance their budgets. In more prosperous times, many states made commitments to lower taxes, higher education spending, and more support for Medicaid, children's health insurance, and other transfer programs. But when the economy turned down, they found themselves faced with commitments they no longer had the financial resources to honor.

Economists have long recommended that states create adequate reserve funds to cushion the shocks of periodic recessions on public services, but while most states have rainy day funds, those funds are usually not big enough to ride out even a modest recession.

So, which commitments take priority? Some states raised taxes, which had a further dampening effect on consumer demand. More cut services to balance their budgets. The state's commitments to smaller classes, less crowded prisons, support for public higher education, and/or access to health care for the state's poor had to be re-examined in the light of scarce resources.

Credible commitment is most important when the program, or the tax policy, or the service affects long-term decisions of individuals. Governments need to pick and choose their commitments. They need to limit their promises to those to which they can reasonably commit themselves and their successors in fiscally responsible ways.

15ᵀᴴ—Martin Luther King Jr.: Prophet of Nonviolence

On the third Monday in January we honor the memory of Dr. Martin Luther King Jr. with a federal and state holiday. We have many ways of honoring his memory, each of which celebrates an aspect of Dr. King's dream for a better world. Some communities focus on racial equality. Others organize volunteer service days in accordance with the National Day of Service that honors Dr. King's famous query: "What are you doing for others?" Communities sometimes celebrate a day of active nonviolence in acknowledgement of his commitment to peaceful resolution of conflict. It is Dr. King as an advocate and practitioner of nonviolence as a philosophy and a way of life that this essay honors.

As a society, America has a tendency to violence. We have higher rates of gun ownership and murder than most developed nations. We like violent sports and violent movies. But there are many Americans who practice nonviolence as a way of life.

Nonviolence is more than the absence of violence. It is not passive. It's a way of life, a conscious refusal to rise to the bait, an attitude toward other people, other parties, and other countries. Nonviolence is hard work. It's going the second mile, not seeking revenge, not exacting an eye for an eye or a tooth for a tooth. Nonviolence begins in attitude. Gandhi, the most successful proponent of change through nonviolent resistance, says that "It takes a fairly strenuous course of training to attain a mental state of nonviolence…Nonviolence is a weapon of the strong."

Nonviolence calls for an attitude of collaboration, of partnership, of acknowledgement of our shared humanity, shared interests, and shared desires. Best/worst, right/wrong, win/lose, conquest/defeat are dichotomies that have a place in the world—to spur us to be and do our best—but they can be a source of great harm when they creep into segments of our lives that should be grounded in mutuality and right relationship.

American society places a high value on competition. Competition spurs us to do our best, to succeed, to win, and in the process, to produce benefits for others. We compete in school for grades and prizes. We compete for entrance into good colleges and for the best-paying jobs when we graduate. We compete on reality shows and game shows to win big money, to be the next Iron Chef or the biggest loser. We compete vicariously through our favorite sports teams or political candidates. We compete as a nation to be the richest, the most successful, the envy of all other nations. But in many aspects of our lives, we rely on collaboration rather that competition to get the results we want. Families, churches, neighborhood associations, food co-ops, and many other ways of organizing to provide for a group or a community downplay competition in favor of everyone contributing what they can to the shared purpose and all being entitled to benefit equally. We depend on other people to help make things happen, and they depend on us, even in the workplace, where teamwork has become an important management principle. So for most of us, both competition and collaboration play important roles in our lives.

The market economy relies on competition as a way to harness our aggressive and individualistic inclinations to the service of the greater good. Our individual pursuit of success and profit under the discipline of competition benefits the economy as a whole. Unlike warfare or other kinds of aggressive behavior, market competition is generally not violent, at least not physically violent.

For economists, the opposite of competition is not collaboration or cooperation but monopoly. Being a monopolist means no longer having to compete, because you have wiped out the competition. You don't have to cater to the consumer, because you have no competition. If people want electricity or water (two typical monopolies) they have to come to you, and they have to pay your price. There are lots of local monopolies as well—the only grocery store in a small town, for example, which charges higher prices because it's so far to the next supplier.

Most economists think that monopolies are short-lived. People will search out substitutes. Eager entrepreneurs will find a way in, a way to break off some segment of the monopolist's market with a different but related product. Competition will find a way. Federal Express and United Parcel Service succeeded by challenging parts of the United States Postal Service monopoly. The American auto industry, long dominated by the big three, found that foreign producers could invade that cozy club with cheaper, better, smaller cars. We are still seeing the consequences of competition in that area of the economy for the former monopolists.

Economists have made careers of studying monopolies, but they have paid surprisingly little attention to the other alternative to competition. Cooperative production of goods and services, according to mainstream economic theory, will usually break down because people will be tempted to free-ride. Free riders are those who enjoy the benefits of shared goods and services without providing their fair share of the effort and funds it takes to produce those goods. Whether it's a food co-op, a sailing club, a church, or some other voluntary cooperative organization, mainstream economics says there will always be shirkers who enjoy the benefits without paying their fair share and thus, eventually, make the voluntary system break down. Yet these collaborative organizations continue to thrive and prosper alongside their more traditional counterparts, the corporation and the for-profit firm.

Some shared goods and services benefit payers and nonpayers alike, like fireworks displays or public beaches or national defense. That's one reason so many shared goods are provided by governments. Another reason is that some goods are just too expensive for low income households to provide for themselves, so they depend on the contributions of others. These goods include affordable housing, transportation, and basic health care. These are government programs, but there's a surprising amount of private effort that goes into making such services available. Despite the predictions of economists, people care about the well-being of others, even strangers, and there are examples everywhere we look of people cooperating to make sure that needs are met.

There are also what economists call club goods, which are provided by voluntary associations such as golf clubs, sailing clubs, singing groups, community theater. Club goods are shared among members and sometimes (usually for a fee) non-members. Producing these kinds of goods and services is more about self-interest than altruism, because it's more fun to sail or sing or act with a group than by yourself. These organizations are pretty good at ensuring that everyone pays their fair share and excluding non-payers.

Another aspect of collaboration that takes some economists

by surprise is that many people do both—they compete and collaborate; they pursue self-interest and contribute to the well-being of others. The same woman who is a profit-maximizing," greedy capitalist" at work may give blood on the way home or pound nails for Habitat for Humanity on the weekend. Human beings are more complex than simple, individualistic, self-interested competitors. We value community in many forms—neighborhoods, voluntary associations, cities, extended families, churches—and many if not most of us are willing to do our fair share to ensure that community-based organizations continue to exist.

Several studies of economic behavior have borne out the notion that our interaction with others is complex and often involves both competition and collaboration. Economics shares with mathematics and psychology an interest in game theory as a way to understand how people interact with each other. One of the findings from game theory experiments is that when people have regular and repeated interactions with others—neighbors, merchants, service providers—they pursue a strategy called Tit for Tat. If you cooperate with me the first time, or treat me fairly, I will do the same to you the next time. If you take advantage of me the first time, I will take advantage of you the next time. The most successful players of these games, which mimic real life, do unto others as they have been done unto in the previous encounter. Eventually a pattern sets in of refusing to play again with those who act purely selfishly, while surviving players collaborate for the best shared outcome. In real life, collaboration means doing your fair share of the work or contributing your fair share of the money even if no one is checking up on you. Selfish behavior may succeed in the short run, but it seldom does in the long run.

How do we as a society balance the benefits and costs of competition by encouraging more cooperative ways of relating to each other? We return to Dr. King, who was not an economist, but a theologian. Theologians and other philosophers help us to shape our understanding of the world and our place in it by calling us to our better selves. In the process, they shave off some of the rough edges of a competitive world. Within the framework of those positive values, habits, and self-understandings, economics can be used to harness competition and encourage collaboration to give us the best of both worlds—the productive economy and the supportive community.

 # FEBRUARY

2ND—GROUND HOG DAY: PUNXATAWNEY PHIL AND ECONOMIC FORECASTING

Groundhog Day is a remnant of an earlier Celtic holiday called Imbolc, which celebrates the promise of the coming spring. Every February 2nd, reporters gather in Punxatawney, Pennsylvania, to see whether the groundhog sees his shadow when he emerges from his hole. A shadow means six more weeks of winter; no shadow forecasts an early spring. The groundhog is a loyal and amusing, if somewhat inaccurate, medium-term weather forecaster. Most of the weather forecasts we rely on for making our daily and weekly plans are short term (up to five days). They predict temperatures as well as rain, wind, sunshine, clouds, and occasionally hurricanes or tornadoes. But Punxatawney Phil and his chief competitor, the Old Farmers' Almanac, make longer term forecasts—Phil for six weeks and the Almanac for the entire year. Weather has economic importance to all kinds of providers of goods and services—farmers, airlines, and tourist services being chief among them.

The patterns of El Nino and La Nina in the Pacific Ocean offer some guidance for these longer term weather forecasts, but only professional meteorologists and atmospheric physicists attempt the daunting task of forecasting years ahead, not merely weather but also climate and climate change.

Economists have a similar challenge in making short-term, medium-term, and long-term economic forecasts. There is a demand for short-term forecasts—GDP, retail sales, stock market indices, and interest rates—that parallels our interest in daily weather forecasts. There is profit to be made in correctly anticipating changes in key variables that affect stock prices, credit availability, the housing market, auto sales, and other important measures of economic activity. That kind of short-term forecasting has an entire industry of its own.

For the medium-term (approximately six months to two years ahead), economists have developed elaborate computer models that predict the behavior of output, employment, prices, and interest rates based on past experience. A collection of leading indicators, including building permits, changes in the money supply, and other variables, has a history of moving about six months ahead of changes in GDP and is a widely used and simple forecasting tool. An uptick or downturn in this index suggests a similar uptick or downturn in GDP six months or so into the future.

While many economists either follow or create short- to medium-term forecasts, relatively few economists make long-term forecasts, the equivalent to the atmospheric scientists' climate change forecasts. While there have always been voices from the margins who predict dramatic, long-term economic changes, mainstream economics is much more likely to predict that more distant tomorrows will be pretty much like today. In fact, that appears to be the way most of us, economists or not, do our personal forecasting—tomorrow will be much like today, only partly modified by recent and current events such as higher unemployment, lower interest rates, or sinking home prices. That gradual adjustment of expectations about the future is called adaptive expectations.

The alternative model, known as rational expectations, is based on the assumption that the average individual is fully informed, rational, and calculating, continuously updating his or her expectations based on new information. This highly economic being is never taken by surprise and is always ahead of the curve, whether around the curve there is a financial market crisis, a housing bubble, a rise or fall in interest rates or the value of the dollar, or other important economic changes. But even this rational being has a somewhat limited time horizon.

The Nobel Prize in Economics has been awarded to scholars on both sides of the question. Economist Robert Lucas, one of the best-known exponents of the rational expectations model in macroeconomics, won the prize in 1995. Herbert Simon, best known for his theory of bounded rationality, received the prize much earlier, in 1978, for propounding a different view. Simon believed that real people acquire and process only limited information in many aspects of their economic lives, which makes them somewhat less than the amazing calculating machine of rational expectations. In 2002, one-half the Nobel Prize in economics was actually awarded to a psychologist, Daniel Kahneman, for his work in determining how people make decisions that are not consistent with the rational economic actor model.

While the rational expectations model is useful, particularly for specific models and short time periods, actual human beings typically choose to invest minimal time gathering and processing economics information. Also, they are influenced by such factors as risk avoidance, framing (the way in which information is presented), and crowd psychology (like the belief that stock prices and/or home prices can continue rising forever), none of which tends to result in rational decision making.

The current economic crisis was forecast by a few of those voices from the margins, but it took most of us, including economists and forecasters, by surprise. The normal ups and downs of economic activity (the business cycle) run in about eight year cycles, which are overlaid by unusual events: the oil price hike and double digit inflation of the 1970s, the stock market/dot.com bust of a decade ago, and the housing market collapse over the past two years, to name a few. Every time we come through a recession, it takes only a short time to assure ourselves and one another that we have learned from the experience and won't repeat it. Then we resume our normal economic lives until the next recession hits.

As Santayana observed, "Those who cannot remember the past are condemned to repeat it." If there is a lesson about forecasting in Groundhog Day, it is one of caution. When Punxatawney Phil fails to see his shadow, we believe it is a promise that winter is over, but shadow or no shadow, we should count on winter coming back again next year.

14ᵀᴴ—Valentine's Day: Heartless Capitalism?

February is named for Juno Februa, the Roman queen goddess in the fever of love. The month falls at the time of year when the earth is wakening to spring, fertility, and new life. Amongst gods and humans, at least, this typically means love and romance, which we celebrate on the 14th day of February. Although Valentine's Day is named for one of several early Christian martyrs by that name, there is no known connection between any of these martyrs and romantic love, so it is the Roman tradition for the entire month that reaches "fever" pitch on Valentine's Day.

It's hard to find much economics in this light-hearted, romantic holiday, celebrated mainly by lovers and children. Economics is not light-hearted. According to economist Alan Blinder, it is either hard-hearted or soft-hearted, but it leans in the hard-hearted direction. In his 1987 book *Hard Heads, Soft Hearts*, Blinder argues that the Republicans are the party of hard heads and hard hearts, the Democrats soft heads and soft hearts. What we need, he argues, is hard heads and soft hearts, combining the practicality and efficiency of the Republican Party and the compassion of the Democratic Party.

A policy or a party that affirms hard heads, hard hearts, is focused on economic incentives. Profits encourage investment, innovation, and risk taking. Higher wages attract more and better workers into jobs and encourage more productivity. If we make it too easy for people to get by with little effort, productivity and output will decline and we will all be worse off. Recent studies of unemployment and unemployment benefits seem to affirm this view of how people behave. Extended unemployment benefits, low as they are, encourage people to wait longer. Typical workers find jobs just as their extended unemployment benefits are running out. True, there are still more than six unemployed workers for every job opening right now, but competition for jobs will ensure that the workers who are hired are productive, hard-working, and well-qualified. It is, after all, competition that drives each of us to be our best. That doesn't mean that we shouldn't make some provision for those who are unable to work—the elderly, children, and the disabled. But we need to be careful to limit unemployment benefits to those who are genuinely unable to make some contribution to productivity, output, and growth.

A policy that affirms soft heads and soft hearts puts more emphasis on quality of life, interdependence, and sharing in one another's gains and losses, risks and rewards. If that sounds like socialism, it is and it isn't. Socialism implies public ownership of the means of production, and very few Americans would support that idea. A more accurate term for a system with more extensive transfer programs or social safety nets is a social welfare state. Most European countries would fit that description. They have high unemployment rates (although most are lower than the United States right now) and generous social welfare programs, including public pensions, day care, health care, and unemployment benefits. They also pay higher taxes to support those welfare programs. Surprisingly, most Western European countries are still quite productive in terms of output, investment, and economic growth, although many of them have followed the same fiscal path into unsustainable borrowing that the United States did.

The choices that a nation makes along the hard-soft continuum are culturally determined, not dictated by economics. It's not the inherent heartlessness of capitalism but the values of citizens in capitalistic countries that determine each country's social policies. Americans historically have emphasized personal freedom, independence, responsibility, and self-reliance as cultural values, and these values are reflected in our limited social welfare programs. We admire those who work hard (a trait we share with the Japanese) and make cultural icons of those who are financially successful in a highly competitive environment. We may argue that our particular brand of social policy is the best in economic terms of competition, incentives, and productivity, but the fact that it works is partly because Americans respond to economic incentives in ways that are influenced by our individualistic, competitive culture.

Even the American emphasis on growth of output, productivity, and innovation as the primary measures of economic performance is driven by cultural values. Other societies have chosen to emphasize a different economic value, such as sustainability, leisure, or equality, even if that choice means a slower rate of growth of output. China, which has become more capitalistic than most Western countries, has made a sudden and dramatic shift recently toward environmental responsibility even at the cost of output and economic growth. European workers take some of their compensation in more extended vacation time. Canada has managed to combine a social welfare state with a highly productive economy. While its per capita GDP is somewhat lower, Canada has a higher life expectancy at birth and a larger share of income accruing to the lowest 20 percent of households than the United States. The tiny nation of Bhutan actually calculates a measure of Gross National Happiness. According to the King, "gross national happiness is more important than gross national product" because "happiness takes precedence over economic prosperity in our national development process."

It's easy to confuse the nature of a market economy with the way it works in one's own culture. A market economy simply means that productive resources are largely privately owned and most economic decisions are made by individuals pursuing their own self-interest. That's true of almost all economies in the world at present. The share of decisions made collectively through government can vary. There will also be differences in the degree of protection extended to all citizens against risks like disasters, medical crises, disability, and unemployment. Market economies are not inherently hard-hearted or soft-hearted. Their heads are usually hard, but the hearts are hardened or softened by the culture of the nation in which the market goes about its daily task of providing food on our tables, roofs over our heads, and opportunities to contribute and to share in the wealth of a productive economy.

- FEBRUARY -

3ʳᴅ MONDAY—PRESIDENT'S DAY: WHAT MAKES A LEADER?

This Monday holiday and three day weekend replaced the celebration of Lincoln's February 12th birthday and Washington's February 22nd birthday with a blended holiday that falls on the 3rd Monday in February, squarely between the two. The Father of Our Country, first in war, first in peace, first in the hearts of his countryman, now shares a day with the Great Emancipator, the first Republican President, and the last casualty of the Civil War. While it's a lot to celebrate on a single day, it is perhaps fitting, as both men are larger-than-life heroes, the stuff that myths are made of. They are both part of the unattainable standard by which we judge our presidential candidates as we go through the interminable process of first selecting the two major candidates and then making a choice between them.

Economist Kenneth Boulding wrote many years ago that there is a sharp contrast between heroic man and economic man. Because he wrote back in the days when "man" was understood to mean "person", I'm going to stick with his language, even though the fashion has become more inclusive. Heroic man makes big choices. Economic man makes little choices. Heroic man has firm principles from which he will not waver. Economic man, weighing at the margin, is a pragmatist; he is willing to think that half a loaf is better than none. Heroic man sees the world in terms of dualism: good/bad, right/wrong. Economic man sees a complex continuum where the choices are less likely to be good or bad, right or wrong, but simply better or worse. Heroic man worries about the slippery slope: raising one tax or allowing abortion in cases of rape opens the door to more tax increases or more allowable abortions. Economic man believes, rightly or wrongly, that rational, calculating adults in positions of authority can define how far they are willing to go and stretch it no farther.

Heroic man does well on the campaign trail, because he is firm, certain, grounded, principled, brave, courageous, and bold. He reminds us of TV's Wyatt Earp and the Lone Ranger. All of us aspire to be like him, to know what we stand for and to be firm in the face of opposition. Making policy, however, is a messy business that requires compromise in order to accomplish anything. Thus, if he can survive the election process, economic man does better at governing. Few of us aspire to be that pedestrian, plodding, and dull, but tweaking and compromising, and making non-heroic choices is the stuff of daily life, whether one is a politician, a cab driver, a banker, or a stay-at-home mom. It is worth noting that while we have elected many lawyers and military heroes to public office, we have elected very few economists.

Elections—especially Presidential elections—are about values and vision. They highlight the difference between how we perceive the state of the nation and what we would like to see as the state of the nation under new (or continuing) leadership. Unfortunately, the focus on the heroic (or non-heroic) qualities of the individuals running for President often distracts our attention from the challenges, opportunities, and public issues each candidate is likely to address while in office. Perhaps, in addition to seeking the heroic man, we should look for the economic man, a leader with the qualities required to implement the vision and address the issues effectively.

Returning to our Presidents' Day honorees, let us consider the leadership qualities Washington and Lincoln possessed. Today we remember Washington mainly for his role in the American Revolution and Lincoln for the Emancipation Proclamation, both heroic acts. But in Washington's eight years in office and Lincoln's just over four years, most of their time was taken up with more mundane decisions and actions that shaped the course of our national life. Both were excellent communicators. Both had the ability to grasp complex issues and to understand what is at stake for all the affected parties. Certainly Lincoln, with a cabinet full of his former political opponents, exemplified the ability to listen and to ferret out the underlying values in what he heard. Washington's daily choices defined the presidency for decades to come, a presidency without the trappings of royalty, a working position accountable to the people. To his great sorrow and regret, Lincoln presided over a civil war and had to make hard choices about the draft and military leadership. Important decisions like the Land Grant Act for higher education and the National Banking Act setting up a more secure financial system were going on during the Civil War—not heroic choices, but important ones. Each time we go through the process of electing a president, we need to be mindful that we need someone capable of both the heroic acts necessary to implement our shared vision and the attention to detail and ability to compromise necessary to deal with the daily choices that face the nation in the years to come.

MARCH

17ᵀᴴ—St. Patrick's Day: Snakes and Ants

Saint Patrick, the patron saint of Ireland, is famous for bringing Christianity to the Emerald Isle and for ridding it of snakes. (Some skeptics believe that there never were snakes in Ireland and that the legend refers to his driving out the Druids, for whom the snake was a symbol.) In addition to Ireland, Saint Patrick is the unlikely patron saint of the small city of Loiza, Puerto Rico. When in the 18th century an infestation of ants threatened to wipe out the yucca plant, the local Catholic parish of Loiza cast lots for a saint to whom they could pray to rid them of the pestilence. The lots fell on Saint Patrick. Most people in Loiza had never heard of him, but they cast twice more, and each time it came up Saint Patrick. So they prayed to Saint Patrick, and the ants disappeared. Their local church is now called the Church of Saint Patrick and the Holy Spirit.

It is interesting to consider in today's world of conservation the idea of celebrating someone for eradicating a species. Since the time of Saint Patrick, we have learned the hard lesson of extinction and near extinction, and the complex chain of unintended consequences that come from plucking something—predator or prey—from the ecosystem. Snakes likely never lived in Ireland and ants continued to thrive in Puerto Rico. If, in fact, Saint Patrick had altered the local ecosystems thus, there would have been consequences of driving away the snakes and ants—probably unchecked growth in the population of nuisance species in Ireland and large changes in the food chain in Puerto Rico.

As we learn more about the interdependence of living beings in the ecosystem, we have become more aware of the unforeseen risks from eliminating any particular species, whether through human carelessness or intent. Deforestation in the tropical rain forests has probably cost us many species of plants and animals, and many of the plants in particular have potential medical uses. The removal of the wolf from the American west led to elk and deer overpopulation which led to deforestation of riverbanks which led to erosion. Today, endangered species get special protection in order to promote their survival. Some species have made a comeback, like the California condor and the buffalo, while others, like the cheetah, remain on the brink of extinction. Some protection efforts, however, have had their share of unintended consequences. Again and again, human activity has been affected in ways that cost jobs and limit our use of valuable resources. Just ask the loggers in the northwest about the spotted owl and the neighbors of the snail darter in Tennessee, where this tiny species held up the construction of the Tellico dam.

Laws regarding endangered species illustrate the law of unintended consequences. Politicians pass laws and regulations, change the tax code, and introduce new programs, and they pat themselves on the back for having done a good thing. Only later do we discover the unanticipated consequences—some good, some not so good. The consequence of property tax relief in many states in the last 20 years has been a significant loss of education funding and pressure on state budgets when the next recession came along. The consequence of bank deregulation in the 1980s and 1990s will be with us for some time to come. Humans do not have perfect foresight, so we pass laws that seem to be eminently sensible or at least harmless at the time, only to lead to harmful consequences years and sometimes decades later.

The same is true of laws that permit the importation of alien species. Today, invasive, non-native species are often blocked from importation to countries where they have no natural enemies. But this hasn't always been the case. Man's movement around the globe has resulted in many sanctioned but in hindsight unfortunate introductions, include rabbits in Australia, Asian carp in the Great Lakes, and pythons in Florida. And it's not just animals. Melaleuca trees in the Everglades have been sucking up water at an excessive rate ever since they were introduced decades ago, and their spread is nearly impossible to control. Ask any Southerner about kudzu, a Japanese import.

Law and economics have a love-hate relationship. Laws provide the framework within which we operate. Laws ensure that contracts will be enforced, rights will be protected, and order will mostly prevail. But laws tend to have an absolute quality, at least as they are written. They are either-or, yes-no, permit/forbid. Economists tend to approach conflicts more in terms of case-by-case decisions, weighing costs and benefits, looking for win-win outcomes and negotiated settlements. They may try to offer incentives rather than pass regulations to protect endangered species, or penalties rather than forbidding imported plants and animals. Perhaps the endangered species can be coaxed into an alternative or narrower habitat. Perhaps we can confine the alien species in a way that keeps it from wreaking havoc with a fragile ecosystem and learn from the experience to more effectively regulate imports of new species with unknown risks.

In a democratic market system, there is a valued place for both approaches to conservation: the absoluteness of law and the case-by-case approach of economics. As we wear the green on March 17th, so close to the spring equinox, we know that the color represents not only Saint Patrick and Ireland but also the green of spring and the natural environment. We depend on our habitat, and we need to protect it, through both laws and thoughtful choices about how we co-exist with the other species with which we share this green earth.

- March -

20ᵀᴴ/21ˢᵀ—Vernal Equinox: Our Fancy Turns to Better Mousetraps

The vernal equinox falls on or around March 20th. An equinox occurs twice a year, when the tilt of the Earth's axis is neither away from nor towards the Sun, because the center of the Sun is in the same plane as the Earth's equator. The vernal equinox is also the marker by which the date of Easter is determined, making Easter a moveable feast. It falls on the first Sunday after the first new moon after the vernal equinox. Probably because of this close association, many ancient customs have migrated from equinox to Easter. The new Easter outfit has its origin in the ancient practice of putting on new clothes to mimic the snake shedding its skin, and Easter bunnies are reminiscent of those very fertile rabbits sacred to the Norse goddess Freya the Fair. Ancient pagans greeted the spring equinox at sunrise, just as Christians now greet their risen Lord at sunrise on Easter.

The vernal equinox, which marks longer days and a warmer season, is a time of rebirth and renewal. It is a time to create and be creative, just as nature is being creative—and procreative!—all around us. Brimming with newness and possibility, the vernal equinox is a great time to think about invention and innovation.

Invention means creating or discovering something new. It can be big, with multiple applications and uses, like lasers or the internet, or a smaller improvement in something already around, like compact fluorescent bulbs to replace incandescent ones. An invention doesn't have to be a tangible product. It can be a work of art or music that is different, a new idea about management, a more effective teaching technique, or a better way to lose weight, rake leaves, or potty train your child.

Invention is usually accomplished by individuals or small teams of individuals. We as a society try to encourage invention by granting exclusive rights to the inventor for a period of time through patents, copyrights, and other forms of protection for original ideas. But it's hard to keep imitators from making minor modifications, from song parodies to better paper clips, that get around these protections. So inventors have to fight a continuing battle to earn a profit on their creations. The internet has made it even easier to steal, borrow, plagiarize, or otherwise take advantage of someone else's creative work without compensation. Cases like Napster and Google and Mega Upload have won some small victories for writers and musicians, but it remains an uphill battle.

For many inventions, there's a gap between the new idea and the practical application. Filling that gap is the process of making the idea commercially feasible and ready to compete in the marketplace. That transition process is called innovation. Innovators put inventions to work; they help inventors earn a profit from selling the product or service to potential customers. Invention can be solitary or interactive, but innovation almost always requires teamwork, because specialized skills are needed to produce and market products, services, ideas or creative works. You may write great songs or design great mousetraps, but you still need someone to produce your CD or build large numbers of mousetraps and someone else to help you market the final product.

This kind of interdependence applies to most of what we create or produce. It allows us to earn a living or make a profit when we sell our goods or services (including our labor services). Most of us produce very little of what we consume—food, housing, electricity, health care, transportation, clothing, and so on. We depend on others to produce it for us in exchange for what we produce. But our interdependence is not limited to consumption. Most of us also depend on a team or organization or firm of some kind to provide us with an opportunity to contribute to production. It's not just sports teams that engage in joint production—it's factories, service firms, schools, or just about anything else that creates value. We have even taken to teaching the art and science of teamwork in school from kindergarten through M.B.A. programs.

While we know a lot about the value of teams and teamwork, we don't have a good clear answer to the question of how we share the profits (or losses) when the product or service is the result of a team effort. We do know that part of the answer is to recognize, value, and reward the person with the creative idea. Some of the credit and some of the profit, however, also belong to the members of the team that translate the idea into a marketable product or service.

In a communist system, the rule for distribution is "from each according to his abilities, to each according to his need." But that system doesn't provide the incentives and rewards that are an essential part of a market system. So in a pure market society, the answer to the question about distribution would be, "to each according to the value of his (or her) contribution." Sometimes we can determine how much more output or sales results from adding one more worker, and pay accordingly. That's what economists call the value of marginal product. Some organizations reward team members through profit-sharing systems or year-end bonuses. Whatever the system, it's important to ensure that everyone, from the idea person to the delivery truck driver, is compensated fairly for his or her contribution. If everyone shares in the firm's success, everyone feels appreciated in a concrete way and has an incentive to work harder and work smarter.

 # APRIL

15TH—INCOME TAX DAY: FLAT AND SIMPLE, OR FAIR AND COMPLICATED?

April 15th is the deadline for filing your federal tax return, and, in many states, your state tax return. Unlike most of the holidays in this series of essays, income tax day is not related to a historical event or the turning of the seasons. It's an arbitrary day chosen by the federal government as a deadline. It is late enough in the year to give people a chance to collect the documents and fill out the forms for the previous year, but early enough to provide the government with some revenue for the second half of the fiscal year, which ends on October 1st.

Americans have been paying federal income taxes since the 16th amendment to the Constitution was ratified in 1913. The original income tax had marginal rates ranging from one percent on the first $20,000 of taxable income to seven percent on income over $500,000. The revenue needs of World War I quickly drove the top bracket rate up to 67 percent on incomes over $2 million. The top bracket rate dropped to 25 percent in the 1920s, only to rise again during the Great Depression. By late in World War II, the top rate was 94 percent on incomes over $200,000. The top bracket rate dropped to 91 percent after the war and stayed there until 1964, when Congress adjusted it to 70 percent. In 1982 the top rate fell again to 50 percent, and in 2001, to 35 percent.

While one would expect the marginal or top bracket tax rate to reflect the amount of tax paid as a percent of income, it doesn't. It isn't even close. In 2011, for example, that top rate of 35 percent only applied to that part of the taxpayer's taxable income (after deductions and exemptions) that exceeded about $380,000. The rest of a taxpayer's taxable income, the first $379,150, was taxed at rates ranging from 10 percent to 33 percent. In 2009, after exemptions, deductions, credits, and applying lower rates to the first parts of income, the average American paid just 11 percent of adjusted gross income in federal income taxes. Even that unpopular top 1 percent paid only a 24 percent average rate.

It's true that the tax code is long and complicated. It's also true that, for the vast majority of taxpayers, it's not that complicated. Families who don't itemize or claim credits for buying new houses or making their existing homes more energy efficient can file quickly and easily. Tax preparers and tax preparation software have further simplified the task of filling out tax returns. Nevertheless, there is a movement to vastly simplify the federal income tax code to the point where it can be filed on a postcard. That proposal is called the flat tax. Economist Alvin Rabushka is credited with developing the idea, but lots of other people have taken it and run with it in various directions.

Most of the proposals for a flat tax are not strictly flat. Typically, these proposals exempt some floor amount of income per household and tax the rest of income at a single flat rate. For a poor household, that exempt amount may be 80 percent or 90 percent of income, so the flat rate would only apply to a small part of income. For a wealthy household, that same exempt amount would be a much smaller share of total income, so the flat rate would apply to most of income. As a result, the poor household would be paying a much lower percentage of total income in taxes than the rich household. So even a flat tax is progressive, although it would be much less progressive than our current system. In an overall state and local revenue system with lots of regressive taxes that hit poor and middle income households harder, there's something to be said for a fairly progressive federal income tax as a balancing factor. Or, maybe simplicity makes it worth giving up that benefit of our present system?

Not necessarily. There's another important complication in going to flat and simple. We would have to give up some cherished deductions and credits. For middle income households, there are three important tax incentives (or what economists call tax expenditures) that would be affected. One is the deduction for mortgage interest and property taxes on homes. Most households figured those deductions into deciding how much home they could afford to buy. Suddenly the deduction is gone! Middle and upper income households also take the tax deduction into account when they make charitable contributions. The higher your marginal rate, the less it costs to give another dollar to charity. Under the flat tax, the charitable deduction would be gone. It's hard to know what the impact would be on charities ranging from churches and colleges to soup kitchens and museums.

The biggest hit for middle income households, however, would come from eliminating the tax exemption for employer-provided fringe benefits, especially health insurance and pension contributions. Fringe benefits typically cost about 30 percent of wages and salaries, so all of a sudden the federal government would assume you were earning 30 percent more for tax purposes. People also save in tax-exempt forms, like 401(K)s and IRAs. These retirement savings would no longer enjoy that tax privilege. A flat tax would discourage saving for retirement and providing health insurance.

The income tax is complicated for a number of reasons. Certainly it is full of loopholes and privileges granted to particular firms and individuals, but it does offset some of the other regressive taxes in the system. It's also a great way for the government to encourage us to do things we should be doing anyway—save for retirement, reduce our carbon footprint, invest in our homes, contribute to charity. So before you join the tax protestors and demand that the income tax be simplified, take a look at your own tax forms and think about what is your fair share to pay and what tax preferences you enjoy and aren't willing to give up.

- *April* -

22ND—EARTH DAY: PROPERTY RIGHTS

On April 22nd we celebrate the Earth and our relationship to it. Earth Day was the brainchild of Senator Gaylord Nelson. It began as a teach-in, a popular form of political activism on university campuses in the 1960s and 1970s. Earth Day is an occasion for celebrating the Earth, protecting the Earth, and enjoying the Earth during the most pleasant season of the year in the northern hemisphere.

Every academic discipline has something to say about the relationship between human beings and the natural world. The field of environmental economics is relatively new. Early economists took the bounty of nature for granted, a source of food and raw materials that made it possible for capital and labor to create goods and services for human consumption. Most of their attention was focused on the scarcity of capital and skilled labor (human capital) as a way to generate growth and a higher standard of living. The founder of modern economics, Adam Smith, titled his monumental 1776 classic *An Inquiry into the Nature and Causes of the Wealth of Nations*. That focus on growth and wealth accumulation has been central to economic inquiry ever since.

As population grew, the seemingly limitless resources of nature began to look more like other scarce resources. Air is not endless, nor can it absorb large amounts of pollutants without deterioration in quality. Competition for scarce water resources and preserving water quality is a challenge in many parts of the world. As forests are bulldozed and prime agricultural land is converted to subdivisions, there is growing concern about whether the planet can sustain the current human population. Loss of wildlife habitat and species diversity, overfishing, loss of soil nutrients, and saltwater intrusion into coastal aquifers are all challenges to human society to rethink our relationship to the Earth.

When resources are abundant—vacant land, water, fishing rights—there is little concern about ownership. But once there are more would-be users of a common property resource than the resource can serve, someone has to judge between the competing claims. Someone has to define, protect, and enforce property rights—the right to buy or sell, the right to use something in a particular way, and the restrictions on that use in order to protect the rights of non-owners. The market is very good at managing the exchange of rights to property, but it cannot define them. Defining, protecting, and enforcing property rights are the most basic functions of government.

The Homestead Act in the early days of the United States offers one example of how governments define property rights. Settlers were moving west in the 19th century in response to the Louisiana Purchase, and someone had to determine who owned particular parcels of land. Families would be reluctant to build a home, start a farm, and make other decisions if they were uncertain about their ability to reap the benefits. They needed not only legal protection of property rights but also military or police protection from the natives they were sometimes displacing and from outlaws of various kinds. In exchange for protection and assurance of the right to the land, the Federal government set down rules about the amount of acreage homesteaders could claim and required settlement for at least five years. The government reserved certain parcels of land to provide shared space for schools, churches, and other communal spaces that would ensure the development of towns. The government also assigned responsibilities to those who received these rights. Today, those responsibilities include not only paying property taxes but also, in many communities, keeping property well-maintained and abiding by zoning restrictions that may prevent residents from raising chickens in the city or building a bowling alley in a residential neighborhood.

Once property rights are defined, if markets are working well and the number of people involved is small, any piece of property should wind up in its highest and best use, regardless of who has the initial ownership claim. If your homestead turned out to be sitting on top of valuable minerals, you could probably be persuaded to sell it and move to another property that doesn't have that advantage. If you want to use a property for farming and someone else wants to build a factory on it, the one who values it the most (indicated by the price offered and accepted) will wind up with the rights to use that property, regardless of who got the initial allocation. This concept is known to economists as the Coase Theorem, and its author, Ronald Coase, won the Nobel Prize in economics for the insight (and other contributions to economics).

Land is not the only scarce natural resource that requires definition of property rights. In the eastern United States, rights to water follow the English riparian tradition, granting the right to use a stream to adjacent owners and the right to underground water to those who live above it. In the west, where water is scarcer relative to demand, there is much more conflict over water rights. Assigned rights to draw on the flow of the Colorado River as it wends its way through multiple states exceed the actual amount of water available. More recently, property rights have been assigned for the use of the air for emissions, embodied in the controversial cap and trade legislation.

Air, and to a lesser degree water, are forms of common property. Because the rights to common property are often not clearly defined or assigned, shared assets tend to take a beating. It's not just air pollution or water pollution or excess withdrawals from a shared watershed. It's the broader idea that everybody's property is nobody's property, so no one has an incentive to take care of it. Common agricultural land is likely to be neglected and over grazed, while private parcels are carefully maintained to ensure maximum yield and sustainability.

When there are competing users or uses for common property, particularly valuable common property, that property needs to have defined ownership. It may be owned by the public, with the government responsible for its management. Or it may be assigned to private owners who then have a financial incentive to maintain it and use it wisely. That insight into the issue of common property resources and competing uses is one contribution from the science of economics that we can celebrate on Earth Day.

 # MAY

1ˢᵀ—May Day: Fertility and Population

May 1ˢᵗ marks the ancient Northern European festival of Beltain, which celebrates the fertility of the Earth and its inhabitants as spring begins to blossom into summer. The maypole is a remnant of that festival. May Day is also an international labor day in many countries, but the holiday we reflect on here is the fertility festival.

Fertility of the Earth is generally regarded as a good thing. Fertility of humans, on the other hand, is a complicated issue with much disagreement over the long-run sustainability of population growth. Economist Julian Simon argued in his book *The Ultimate Resource*[1] that producing more people would expand a productive

---

1   Simon, Julian, *The Ultimate Resource* (Princeton University Press, 1983).

resource that would contribute to output and growth. Critics, including entomologist Paul Ehrlich, author of *The Population Bomb*[2], were alarmed at the possible catastrophic consequences of unchecked human population growth on a planet of finite size and carrying capacity.

The argument over population growth dates back at least to British parson and economist Thomas Robert Malthus, who argued in 1798 that human population grows geometrically (2, 4, 8, 16,...) while the food supply grows arithmetically (1,2, 3, 4, 5...). Why does the food supply grow more slowly? Diminishing returns. As more seeds, fertilizer, tractors, and workers are applied to a limited or fixed supply of arable land, the additional output will grow more and more slowly in response to each increase in inputs. Malthus pointed out that if we could continue to increase output by applying more and more non-land resources to a fixed supply of land, then theoretically we could feed the world out of a flowerpot!

Diminishing returns simply means successively smaller increases in output for each unit of additional input. The idea of diminishing returns has many applications in economics, although this one is the most famous. Adding more and more workers to a factory without increasing the scale of the plant will eventually make the workplace so crowded that it is difficult to move, let alone produce. Long before reaching that point, however, increases in output will be smaller with each extra worker, because of limits on the availability of tools, machines, and other complementary resources.

In the absence of dramatic technological change, Malthus argued, population growth would be checked by famine and

---

2   Erhlich, Paul, *The Population Bomb* (Ballantine Books, 1971).

starvation and disease unless people could be persuaded to take steps to control their fertility. One prescription for this dismal projection is population control. While birth control is controversial in many places, modern methods of family planning have made it easier for families to limit the number of children they have. In fact, the availability of both birth control and abortion has reduced fertility rates below the replacement level in some countries, particularly Russia.

The other possibility for keeping up with population growth is to increase output so as to provide for the additional guests at the table. Technological change, especially in food production, has certainly postponed some of the more dire predictions of collapse. The Green Revolution, for example, led to large increases in agricultural productivity in the 1970s, although agronomists are now observing that many of these gains in output were at the cost of sustainability. The new varieties of staple crops are more dependent on petroleum based fertilizer, large scale production, and pesticides than some of the older varieties grown by peasant farmers on small plots for centuries. The loss of plant species diversity also makes crops more vulnerable to insect pests and disease. More recently, the debate has shifted to the possibilities that come with genetically modified crops, weighing the risks and benefits associated with foodstuffs that are the products of engineering and chemistry.

The argument over increasing the food supply versus controlling population is not easily resolved, because both positions are rooted in particular economic ideologies that offer differing interpretations of the facts. The facts include not just the successes and shortcomings of the Green Revolution and the potential for further technological innovations that will enable agricultural production to transcend those limitations. There are also the challenges of climate change, soil erosion, water shortages, and other limitations on how many humans this planet can support. The neoconservative position, dominant among contemporary economists, is that a combination of technological improvements and market forces should enable humans to expand the availability of potable water, food, and other resources to meet the needs of all without dramatic change or significant government intervention. They also point to declines in fertility that occurred in the industrial world as first the death rate fell with improved sanitation, nutrition, and health care, and then the decline in the need for large numbers of children to work the farm and support couples in their old age. This trend in developing countries should slow and ultimately stabilize human population. The only question is: How soon will it happen?

An alternative world view was expressed in a book called *The Limits to Growth*,[3] published in 1972 with an update in 2004. The authors are skeptical about the potential for technological change and voluntary population control to offset the reality of finite resources. Because the market is not always the most effective tool for addressing the need for coordinated action, they believe government intervention is needed. It is true that in a young, underpopulated country, the benefits of population growth are likely to exceed the drawbacks. More people means a critical mass of workers for more labor-intensive methods of production and an adequate market to support the production and sale of goods and services that have economies of scale. There will be more opportunities to specialize, which will increase efficiency. But once population

---

3   Meadows, Donella *et.al.*, *The Limits To Growth* (Signet, 1972). An update, called *Limits to Growth: The 30-Year Update* (Chelsea Green Publishers) was published in 2004.

reaches a certain size, the costs of further population growth begin to appear, including noise, crowding, and growing shortages of certain kinds of essential resources such as potable water, fossil-fuel based energy, clean air, and arable land. The market solution of rising prices to allocate these scarce resources can leave those at the bottom of the income distribution to fend for themselves in an increasingly Malthusian world.

Which view of human population growth is correct? Only time will tell.

2ND SUNDAY—MOTHER'S DAY: ALL MOTHERS ARE WORKING MOTHERS

The second Sunday in May is known in the United States as Mothers' Day, while in the United Kingdom it is called Mothering Sunday. By either name, it is a day to celebrate our own mothers and motherhood in general. It has had that slot on the calendar since it was first proclaimed in 1914.

Mothers' Day began in an era when most married women, and especially married women with children, did not work outside the home. Today the majority of American women are in the labor force. The number of women working outside the home has grown dramatically in the last 40 to 50 years. The prime age (25-54) labor force participation rate for women with children more than doubled between 1960 and the present, slightly offsetting a decline in labor force participation by men. Increased education for women, smaller families, and a higher divorce rate all contributed to this trend. Women's labor force participation rates are now comparable to those for men.

In 2011, 77 percent of mothers of children under age 18 were in the labor force. Even mothers of very young children (under age 3) have a 60 percent labor force participation rate—that is, they are either working or actively seeking work. These women hold down two jobs—their paying occupation and the nonpaying job of mothering. The labor force participation rate for mothers with children under age 18 is actually higher than for women in general, because older women are less likely to be working, some because they never worked outside the home, others because they have retired after working at an earlier stage of life.

While women and men are now working outside the home in equal numbers, women generally earn less than men. According to the United States Department of Labor, in 2011 women who worked full-time earned about 77 percent of what men earned. The earnings gap was even smaller (89 percent) for women workers ages 25 – 34. That was a substantial improvement over the 1960s and 1970s, when the gap hovered around 60 percent.[4]

Economists have been scratching their heads over this earnings gap for almost fifty years. Women and men do make different job choices. In recent decades, however, many more women have chosen traditionally male occupations such as medicine, law, science, and engineering. This movement of women into traditionally male occupations has narrowed the gap between men's and women's earnings. Even within occupations, however, there are earnings differences that favor male workers. Some of the difference is due to interruptions in work history. But maternity leaves have become shorter, and women are having fewer children than in earlier decades, so that source of earnings differentials has declined.

Most statistical studies are able to explain part of the wage gap in terms of occupational choice, interrupted work history, and other factors. But even as the wage gap has narrowed, these studies all leave some part of the differences in earnings between men over women unexplained. Psychological studies show that employers and customers prefer males over females in many situations. If such preferences are widespread, they would make an equally qualified woman less likely to be hired than her

---

4   "Highlights of Women's Earnings in 2008," U.S. Department of Labor, U.S. Bureau of Labor Statistics, July 2009, Report 1017.

male competitor. Or, if she is hired, she may be paid less because she is perceived as less productive despite any evidence to the contrary.

Discrimination still exists in the labor market. In part, it's because our cultural perceptions lag reality. The image of Mom at home with the kids and Dad away at work all day is still a large part of our cultural memory, particularly among the more senior employees, who are typically the ones making hiring decisions. The image of males as competitive and women as cooperative, a stereotype with some degree of grounding in reality, also creates a bias against women in occupations where competition is valued more highly than cooperation. Historically, women gravitated toward occupations and academic disciplines in which cooperation or nurturing is highly valued, such as teaching, nursing, and social work. Were these lower paying occupations because they were largely occupied by women, or were women channeled into these occupations because they paid less and were therefore less attractive to men?

To all the challenges of 21st century mothering, moms need to add the challenge of dealing with cultural pressures that push girls and boys in different directions and stereotypes that limit the ability of our daughters to compete on a level playing field and succeed (or fail) on their own terms. No one ever said that mothering was an easy job. (We'll address fathering next month.) That's why it gets a day of its own when we pause to reflect on both the importance of the unpaid work done by mothers and the question of fairness or equity in pay for work outside the home.

JUNE

14ᵀᴴ—FLAG DAY: HOW BIG SHOULD A COUNTRY BE?

June 14th is Flag Day in the United States. Since 1916, Flag Day has commemorated the adoption of the flag of the United States by the Second Continental Congress in 1777. Flag Day is not a national holiday. Banks and government offices are open, and the United States mail delivery takes place as usual. However, many communities celebrate this minor holiday with parades and other festivities, and, of course, it is a grand excuse for a sale at the mall!

Flags are not limited to countries. States, organizations, corporations, and cities have flags of their own. Flying garden flags has become popular in the United States. But national (and state) flags are unique in representing sovereign authority. If you want to find a post office, or a consulate, or a state capitol building, look for the flag (although you may find yourself on the lot of a patriotic auto dealer instead).

National flags come in a variety of sizes, and they are usually rectangular. Countries also come in a great variety of sizes, although they are rarely rectangular. The ancient world gave us two conflicting models of how big a country should be. Empires—Egyptian, Assyrian, Babylonian, Roman—strove to be as big as possible. They absorbed smaller nations and used them as sources of labor, raw materials, and taxes. While later Greeks built an empire too, the early Greeks gave us a different model, the city-state. Loosely federated and often in conflict, the Greek city states, of which Athens and Sparta were the most famous, stayed small because they were governed more or less democratically (Athens more, Sparta less), so they needed a high degree of consensus. Fewer people makes consensus easier to attain. Likewise, the Jewish nation of the Old Testament occupied a small geographic area, with a population that was ethnically and religiously homogeneous. They were less interested in creating empire than in unifying and protecting the space within which they could function as God's chosen people. Historically, the empire model has outweighed the small nation model.

Today the world has more than 200 countries. There are four tiny sovereign nations in Europe (Liechtenstein, Monaco, and San Marino with populations ranging from 30,000 to 35,000, and Vatican City, population 800). At the opposite end are such population giants as China with 1.3 billion people and India with 1.1 billion. The United States is third with about 311 million. In land area, the largest three countries are Russia, Canada, and the United States.

Country size, measured either by population or land area, is a product of history and geography—settlements, wars, oceans, mountains, and other boundaries that separate one group of people from another. Some countries share a long history, a single language, a common culture, and even a gene pool, all of which make its citizens distinctive in their similarity to each other and differences from foreigners. Other countries are a blend of cultures and languages, especially in modern times when transportation and relocation have become mere inconveniences compared with the ordeal they were in earlier periods. But these blended, modern nations, especially those that are democratically governed, face a new challenge: How big and how diverse can we as a nation become and still be able to agree on anything?

There are two important answers to this question; one stems from economics, the other from political science. From economics we turn to the theory of clubs, which addresses the optimal size of a voluntary organization, like a sailing club, or a church, or a neighborhood association—or a city. It's true that we don't necessarily choose to join a country, although we may choose to leave it, and we are more likely to choose our state or city. But the same considerations apply. Increased population adds both benefits and costs to the equation. More people can share the cost of providing public services because new arrivals usually (not always) cost less to serve than they generate in taxes and other public revenue. More people can also create a critical mass to make it feasible to offer certain services, public or private, because the market is large enough to support them. As Adam Smith famously (well, famously among economists) said, "The division of labor is limited by the extent of the market." The bigger the market, the more diversity of products and services we can support and still have the benefits of specialization. The provision of specialized services, like upscale restaurants, tea shops, and specialty stores, demands more consumers than does the corner market.

On the other hand, increased population means more differences in tastes, preferences, and opinions, so there is likely to be increasing dissatisfaction, especially with the public sector. More people can also mean greater diversity in language, lifestyle, religion, and other characteristics, especially if the newcomers arrive from other cultures, and those differences can cause conflict and misunderstanding. So bigger also means a less congenial environment. The optimum population is reached when the additional benefits of one more person or household are just enough to put up with the additional costs. We may not be able to define that number precisely, but the signs of exceeding it are clear—anti-immigrant grumbling, complaints about congestion, disagreements over public decisions.

The second answer to the "How Big?" question comes from political science, and it's a partial solution: Federalism. Federalism means that a large country has not only an encompassing central government and smaller local governments (cities, counties, school districts) but also a middle level. States in the United States, Brazil, Australia, India, and Italy; provinces in Canada; Lander in Germany; cantons in Switzerland all accommodate diversity by creating smaller entities within the larger country which provide the kind of public and private environment that suits their constituency. If you don't like the high taxes and high level of public services in New York, move to New Hampshire. If you think California is too crowded, there's always Montana. States are also good places to experiment with new ideas, like income maintenance programs in New Jersey or different kinds of health insurance schemes in

Oregon and Massachusetts. In a federal system, responsibilities are assigned to levels of government based on where the benefits are concentrated. Streets and garbage pickup benefit the locals, so they are managed at the local level. Graduates of public schools in the United States move around, but are more likely to remain in the state where they grew up, so schools are largely a shared state-local responsibility. At the national level the military protects us all and we enjoy the benefits of a single national currency.

Europe has been struggling with the issue of optimum size for more than fifty years. The European Economic Community of six nations and six currencies that was formed in 1957 grew to the 27 nation giant European Union of 2012, with many but not all member nations sharing the euro as their common currency. In the process of integration, the citizens of a united Europe learned some important things about sovereignty, about how much of their own folkways they would have to give up to be part of the Union, about the costs and benefits of free movement of people and products and firms between countries. Starting in 2011, the debate has been mostly about monetary policy and deficits, about Greece and Italy and the euro, but that's only the latest in a series of challenges that stem from learning to live together in a very large, very powerful sovereign entity with a lot of differences to iron out.

So, as we honor the United States flag on Flag Day, it's a good time to think about how to balance the benefits of bigness with the costs of diversity. It's also a good time to work on getting along better with those who share our flag.

3ʳᴰ SUNDAY—FATHERS' DAY: THE CHANGING AMERICAN FAMILY

Father's Day, which honors fathers and celebrates fatherhood, is celebrated on the third Sunday of June in 52 countries. It was first celebrated in the United States on June 19, 1910. Father's Day is a good time to reflect on the changing American family. Yes, there are still plenty of traditional families—mother, father, 2.3 children—but there are many more nontraditional families than there used to be. Of America's 74 million children under age 18, 70 percent live with both parents, although about 5 percent of those parent pairs are not married. Three-fourths of the remaining 22 million children live with their mothers, 11percent with their fathers, and the remaining 14 percent with neither parent. Increasingly, the neither parent option is one or more grandparents.

There has also been a marked increase in births to unmarried mothers, and not just teens. The stigma of unwed motherhood is gone, and the image of the father as the protector and supporter of the family has waned. But United States social policy, much of it designed in the 1930s, is still based on the concept of the traditional two-parent family where the father is the breadwinner and the mother is at home with the children. Three kinds of social policies in particular are based on that model: welfare, Social Security, and the income tax.

Economists have always dodged the question of whether the appropriate unit to use on matters of consumption and taxation is the individual or the household. Economics is based on the idea of the rational economic man, or rational economic person, pursuing his or her own economic self-interest. But who is that rational economic man, an individual or a married couple? Are household decisions about working, earning, spending, borrowing, and investing made by one person or by a committee? And what about the needs and preferences of the children?

For decades the head of the household, normally the father, stood for the entire household as a taxpayer, earner, and determiner of consumption, even if the wife and mother not only did the shopping but earned money in her own right. Welfare was designed for widows and orphans, not divorcees or unwed mothers. Social Security provided pensions for widows (and occasional widowers) who did not qualify for benefits through work on their own, and also for children of deceased workers under age 18. The federal income tax has never quite figured out how to deal with the two-income household. Joint tax returns (with the option of filing separately) came into being in the late 1940s only because community property states treated income as belonging to both marriage partners even if only one actually worked for pay.

Of the three policies, the program that has made the greatest adaptation to the changing nature of families is welfare. As Aid to Families with Dependent Children (AFDC) was converted to Temporary Assistance to Needy Families (TANF) in the 1990s, there was less focus on whether there was an able-bodied male in the household (which would make the family ineligible for welfare) and more stress on the importance of work for whatever adults were available, even mothers of very young children. Time limits and work requirements have removed many people from the welfare rolls, most of them mothers. The earlier emphasis on "deadbeat dads" and collecting child support has taken a back seat to encouraging self-sufficiency from whichever parent is on the scene, father or mother.

Social Security has a problem that stems from the same source but results in being more generous to traditional families—those in which one spouse, usually the wife, works very little or not at all outside the home. She is entitled to a wife's benefit (50 percent of her husband's Social Security check) as long as her husband is alive and up to 80 percent of his benefits after he dies, as long as her husband worked enough years under Social Security. Payments by both husbands and wives (and single people as well) into the Social Security system go to support these benefits to stay-at-home wives, but neither second earners in a two-adult household nor single persons get any additional benefits.

Finally, the federal income tax has vacillated between defining the taxpayer as an individual earner or as a married couple. Hybrid tax schedules for individuals and married filing separately, married filing jointly, and heads of households (with other dependents but no spouse) have tried to bring some fairness in tax treatment to disparate kinds of family units. Married couples have been a powerful lobby on behalf of what they think is equity in taxation, both in one-earner and two-earner marriages.

For decades economists treated the business firm as a black box that purchases inputs and converts them into outputs, without giving much thought to what went on inside the black box. Starting with Ronald Coase's 1937 "The Nature of the Firm," a whole new way of looking at the inner workings of the firm emerged. Firms can do things that individuals cannot because they can create long-term contracts with workers and supply chains in ways that minimize the costs and wastes of producing goods and services for a profit, compared to other ways of organizing production. But households are also production and consumption decision-making entities, with contracts ranging from prenuptial agreements to informal division of household responsibilities that save the trouble of renegotiating anew every day. Perhaps it's time for economists and social policy makers to take the same kind of close look at the inner workings of the household and to consider how changing roles of husbands and wives, fathers and mothers should be reflected in those policies. Father's Day would be a good time to start.

JULY

July—The Month of Revolutions

It must be the heat, or maybe the humidity. July is not the only month in which revolutions have taken place, but historically it is a politically explosive month. Three of the most famous revolutions are celebrated in July: the American Revolution (July 4th), the French Revolution (July 14th), and the Cuban Revolution (July 26th). While some revolutions spark counter-revolutions, all three of these revolutions had lasting and dramatic impact on the form of government and the future direction of their respective countries. For the thirteen colonies that became the United States, it was a rare but dramatically successful overthrow of a distant colonial power in order to take charge of their own destiny. For the French, the revolution ended an abusive and repressive monarchy but also initiated decades of upheaval, including the Reign of Terror and the rise of Napoleon, before finally settling into a modern democratic state. For Cuba, likewise, the revolution overthrew a repressive dictator, Fulgencio Batista, before evolving into the only long-term communist state in the Western hemisphere. This revolution was named for and is celebrated on its starting date of July 26, 1953, although it wasn't until January 1st, 1959, that the revolutionaries actually took over the government.

Many nations have undergone revolutions—the October Revolution in Russia (1917), the Glorious Revolution in England (1688), and the Mexican Revolution that lasted from 1910 until 1920, to name a few. A revolution is generally a tactic of last resort. Because revolution is both risky and costly in terms of lives lost and damage done, it is seldom attempted unless conditions are really bad and other methods of resolving differences and addressing grievances have failed. From George III in 1776 to Louis XVI to Czar Nicholas III to Porfirio Diaz in early 20th century Mexico to the Arab spring wave of revolutions in the Middle East, the refusal to listen and respond to genuine problems has been costly to those who thought they held absolute power.

The goal of revolutions is almost always a transfer of power from the autocrat of the day to the people. The French Revolution probably wins the prize for the most succinct and appealing slogan— Liberté, Egalité, Fraternité (freedom, equality, brotherhood). That's a lot catchier than "taxation without representation is tyranny."

Freedom was paramount on the minds of the American revolutionaries, and it remains important to Americans to this day, often at the expense of equality and/or brotherhood (or its 20th century Polish equivalent, solidarity or community). For Cubans, equality was the primary goal, which manifested itself in the form of a Communist government that offered little personal freedom to its citizens. The French Revolution never had quite such a clear sense of direction but came closest to brotherhood, or community, in eventually creating a democratic welfare state that attempted to honor both freedom and equality.

The freedom-equality debate is very old and very central to political economy. If we maximize freedom, which includes the freedom to keep the fruits of one's efforts and the freedom to fail, a free economy will also be one of great inequality. If we maximize equality, we lose some of those incentives to work hard, to innovate, to invest that increase the size of the economic pie we all share. In a society that has neither freedom nor equality, like Batista's Cuba or France under Louis XVI, this conflict may not appear to be as critical, because the revolutionaries would like both, or at least one, of these goals to be realized. But in a society that has been democratic for some time, the conflict is very real and not easily resolved. Instead citizens vacillate from pole to pole, focusing on freedom when the economy is strong and turning toward equality during hard times.

Where does that third goal fit into the picture—community, solidarity, brotherhood? Perhaps it is the tie that binds the other two together. If as a nation really is a community, then its citizens have not only freedom but also responsibility to one another. Freedom exercised responsibly by people with a sense of community will ensure that we collectively provide for the less fortunate, create opportunities, and give back to the society that enabled its members to thrive and prosper.

Economics is not about absolutes, but about tradeoffs. A little less freedom in exchange for a stronger sense of community, a little less equality to permit greater freedom. It's not the stuff of revolutions, but rather of evolution, of tinkering, experimenting, responding to situations with a rebalancing of these three revolutionary values. A nation that finds a way to honor all three values and to adapt to changing circumstances by rebalancing among those three values is less likely to experience another violent revolution. So on Independence Day, Bastille Day, and 26 Julio, we celebrate not only the success of our respective revolutions but the importance of the day-to-day balancing act that makes it less likely that the country will need another revolution to get it right.

- *July* -

14ᵀᴴ—Bastille Day: The Costs of Inequality

July 14th marks the anniversary of the 1789 French revolution that toppled the monarchy and began a long period of political instability. That was the day citizens attacked the prison known as the Bastille and liberated the prisoners. Their British neighbors had revolted in the previous century, but they kept a rather domesticated monarchy and shifted the power to Parliament. France would go through several empires, a republic, and a brief restoration of the monarchy before developing a lasting democratic form of government.

The violence of the French revolution was the product of an arrogant, out-of-touch monarchy and dramatic inequalities between the aristocracy and the ordinary citizens of France. Immediately before the revolution, there was widespread famine, unemployment, and a huge national debt resulting from frequent wars. Yet the nobility and the court of Louis XVI and Marie Antoinette engaged in lavishly conspicuous consumption. The intensity of the grievances and the violence of the response make it clear that the French revolution had more in common with the Russian and Cuban revolutions than with the British or American ones.

A system that is both democratic and market-oriented has to be alert to the changing balance between incentives and inequality. In *Equality and Efficiency, the Big Tradeoff,* economist Arthur Okun advocates progressive taxation so that transfers can be made from the rich to the poor. However, he recognizes problems in such an arrangement, which he describes in a colorful metaphor: "The money must be carried from the rich to the poor in a leaky bucket. Some of it will simply disappear in transit, so the poor will not receive all the money that is taken from the rich" (p. 91). The losses result from both administrative costs and from the reduced incentives of both the rich and the poor to work harder and produce more.

While Okun successfully diagnosed the problems associated with reducing inequality, he paid relatively little attention to the challenge posed by increasing inequality, which has been the pattern of the last three decades in the United States and many other countries. According to the Congressional Budget Office, there has been a dramatic increase in inequality of income shares in the United States. After taxes, the lowest 20 percent of the income distribution received 4.8 percent of total income in 2005, while the top 20 percent received 51.6 percent. The top 1 percent alone received 15.6 percent of total after-tax income. Median income in the lowest 20 percent of earners rose only 6 percent (after adjusting for inflation) between 1979 and 2004, while it rose 69 percent for the top 20 percent and a whopping 176 percent for the top 1 percent.

Aside from concerns for the welfare of those at the bottom of the heap, what problems stem from increasing inequality in the distribution of income and wealth? In the private marketplace, in theory, we cast our votes for goods and services with dollars, so those with more dollars have more votes or buying power. But in the public marketplace, in which we select public officials and express our views on issues, we supposedly have a system of one person, one vote. Everyone is equal in the political marketplace.

Many conservatives fear that the more numerous poor will gang up on the smaller number of rich to extract transfer payments. Liberals have the opposite concern, that money will find its way from the private to the public marketplace and be used to buy candidates, elections, policies, and legislation that favor the rich.

Even in the private marketplace, an increasing concentration of income and wealth, combined with laws that protect corporations from accountability to anyone but shareholders, has resulted in an increasing concentration of economic power in a smaller number of large firms. Retail chains such as Walmart, Target, Lowe's, Home Depot, Barnes and Noble, Office Depot, and Staples dominate their respective markets, giving consumers few alternatives and squeezing their suppliers for concessions. Local banks have become local offices of large national banks. Consumer sovereignty—the customer is king—and labor unions are both much weaker in the face of concentrated power and wealth.

In the early years of the 20th century, a combination of antitrust laws and regulatory agencies, such as the Federal Trade Commission and state utility commissions, attempted to limit the power of monopolies. Teddy Roosevelt came to fame in part as a "trust-buster," fighting the monopoly power of Standard Oil, U.S. Steel, and other large firms. During the Great Depression, bank regulation was added to the list; banks were insured by the federal government but required to limit their risk-taking in exchange. But deregulation in the late 20th century undid many of these earlier efforts to control monopoly power that threatened both political and economic democracy.

A much more egalitarian France as well as a pretty egalitarian Canada have weathered the recent global financial and economic meltdown relatively well, unlike their more laissez-faire cousins in the United States and Britain. Both France and Canada kept tighter controls on their financial firms and have a welfare state that offers greater protection to citizens during economic downturns. They also both have less income inequality than the United States and Britain because of higher, more progressive taxes and a more extensive safety net of welfare programs, public services, and unemployment protections (verify). In the wide open, deregulated market economies of the United States and Britain, perhaps the Occupy movement, with its focus on inequality and power, is a signal that the seeds of another revolution are being sown—hopefully a less violent one than the 1789 revolution in France.

 # AUGUST

August—The Month with No Holidays

While there are several minor religious holidays in August, there are no major holidays. Ramadan begins in August some years, but it's on a lunar calendar, so it varies from year to year. The ancient Celtic festival of Lammas, or first harvest, is on August 1st, but you won't find Lammas cards in your local Hallmark store. August just has nothing big—no fireworks, no family gatherings, no cards or gifts, no parades, no patriotic speeches, no excuse for sales at the mall. Sandwiched between the celebrations of the American, French, and Cuban revolutions in July and Labor Day at the beginning of September, August's sole claim to calendar fame lies in being the last chance to get away from it all before children and youth return to school. It's a favorite time for vacations, especially in Europe and North America.

In difficult economic times some families turn to "staycations"—staying home and enjoying local recreation and outdoor adventures. For most vacationers, however, a vacation involves a change of venue, away from the household chores, the neighbors, and the daily routine. Whether it's a nature's paradise of beach, mountains, or a national park, a theme vacation at Disney, a cruise, ecotourism, a week at a luxury condo, or camping out in a state park, the essence of vacation is the three Rs—not reading, (w)riting, and (a)rithmetic, but refreshment, reinvigoration, and renewal.

The word vacation comes from the French word "vacances," which means empty or blank. On the medieval calendar, there were so many religious holidays, fairs, or festivals that the blank dates on the calendar were outnumbered by the celebratory ones. Today it is reversed; the work days on the calendar are filled with meetings and task and commitments, and the blank ones are the holidays.

Medieval Europe was not noted for progress, or productivity, or innovation. What it was noted for was a lot of free time, particularly in the agricultural off-season. For centuries of human life, the rhythm of work and rest, or work and play, was governed by the tasks of an agricultural life and the flow of the seasons. Even today, with only 1.4 percent of our population earning a living in agriculture, the school calendar is still governed by that earlier need for children to be available to help with farm chores in the warm weather. In Central America, the long holiday season still falls in December and January so that children will be available to harvest the coffee crop. The economy still needs seasonal workers—not just migrant farm labor but seasonal tourism workers in destination areas, extra retail workers in November and December, landscape workers in the warm season. But in a world where so much work can be done at any time of year, we have to create an artificial ebb and flow to provide for rest, renewal, and refreshment that not only makes workers more productive but makes their lives more satisfying. Vacation plays an important role in that ebb and flow.

American workers enjoy fewer and shorter vacations than their fellow workers in most other advanced nations, and they are expected to work longer hours in the workweek. Not only are there fewer days away from the job in the year, there are also fewer hours away from the job during the week. United States output per worker is among the highest in the developed world, but output per hour is not. More hours per worker is a primary source of increases in productivity.

The most useful measure for international comparisons among workers is hours worked per year, which reflects not only hours per week but also vacations and holidays. In the United States, that number is 1,797 hours, ranking ninth out of 32 developed nations. Number one is South Korea, at 2,357; number 32 is the Netherlands, at only 1,391 hours a year. Weekly hours vary, but vacation days also contribute to the difference. Workers in the United States typically have 10 days (two weeks) of vacation, while British workers get 20 days (four weeks), and the French 25 (five weeks).[5]

Traditionally, when productivity increases, workers get higher wages per hour, either by getting more pay for the same hours or the same pay for fewer hours. According to the Heritage Foundation, total compensation has kept pace with productivity for the American worker, but the gains have been distributed in the form of increased wages and fringe benefits, rather than shorter

---

5   Olson, Parmy, "The World's Hardest Working Countries," www.forbes.com, MY 21, 2008. Accessed on June 7, 2009.

hours. Most of those gains have gone into fringe benefits.[6] Health insurance premiums for family coverage have risen 113 percent between 2001 and 2011. The cost—averaging $5,429 for single coverage and $15,429 for family coverage—is shared between employer and employee in two ways, the employee contribution to the premium and the increased use of larger deductibles. The average share of that premium paid by employers is 82 percent for single coverage and 72 percent for family coverage.[7]

While some employers offer flexibility in number of hours worked, and many professionals and self-employed workers have some choice about hours worked, most workers have jobs that come with an expectation for the workweek and a set policy on vacations, holidays, and sick leave. So to some extent the longer annual hours and shorter average vacation time for an American worker is an employer choice, shaped partly by cultural factors and expectations but primarily by economic considerations.

For an employer, it is more cost-effective to hire fewer workers and have them work longer hours than to hire more workers, give them more vacation time, and shorten the work week. There is a cost to hiring and training, and hiring fewer workers for longer annual hours reduces that cost, especially in a mobile society where worker turnover is high. But an even more significant factor is fringe benefits, especially those fringe benefits that are a fixed cost per worker rather than a percent of wages. Those fixed cost benefits are cheaper when you spread the cost over the same worker for more hours rather than more workers each of whom works fewer hours.

---

6   www.heritage.org/Research/Labor/wm498. Accessed June 9, 2009.

7   The Kaiser Family Foundation and Health Research and Education Trust, *Employer Health Benefits: 2011 Summary of Findings*, p. 1.

The most important of those fixed benefit costs per worker is health insurance. The United States is one of the few developed nations to rely heavily on employer-provided health insurance. It's something of a historic accident that the United States chose that route rather than a tax-funded system, which might have been a single payer system or one involving private insurers. As far as worker hours and vacations are concerned, the issue is the method of funding, not the method of delivering health care and health insurance. Whether or not the United States converts to a single payer system (like many other countries) or some other way of ensuring universal coverage that maintains a role for private insurers, it is clear that there is a need to rethink this heavy reliance on employer-funded health insurance. A system that depends mainly on employer-provided health care leaves a lot of families out of the system and results in loss of health insurance during unemployment. It also affects those who keep their job and their insurance, because requiring employers to provide health insurance raises labor costs, so wages rise more slowly and fewer workers are hired. Health insurance costs contribute directly to longer work weeks and shorter vacations. Higher United States health insurance costs have also been a factor in some manufacturers locating in Canada, resulting in fewer jobs for American workers.

So next time you are sitting in your cubicle, longing for a few more leisurely days of summer, make the connection. Would you rather pay more taxes for health care and take that extra compensation that now comes as health insurance in the form of higher wages, shorter hours, and/or longer vacations? Or would you rather keep things just the way they are? The 2010 Affordable Care Act, nicknamed Obamacare, didn't tackle the issue of employer-provided health care head on, so the question is still on the table:

Who should pay for health care, employers, the government, the individual, or some combination of the three? It's a tough choice and a difficult arrangement to alter.

 # SEPTEMBER

1ST MONDAY—LABOR DAY: MINIMUM WAGE, LIVING WAGE

The first Monday in September is Labor Day in the United States—unlike most of the rest of the world, where this holiday is celebrated on May 1st. Labor, or work, is a central part of our lives. It provides income to pay for the food on our tables and the roof over our heads. It offers dignity, meaning, and a sense of making a contribution. It may offer companionship and satisfaction. It can also take over our lives and crowd out other meaningful aspects of being human—relationships, hobbies, community involvement, learning, and play. So work and earnings offer a good reflective issue for this end of summer holiday. It seems appropriate on Labor Day to again ask the question posed in the Bible (Luke 10:7): Is the worker worthy of his hire? And also the companion question, less frequently asked: Is the wage worthy of the worker's effort?

In 1957, when I was working my first part-time job as a retail sales clerk, the minimum wage was $1.00 an hour. In 1996 dollars, that was equivalent to $5.58. When it was first enacted in 1938 as part of the Fair Labor Standards Act, the minimum wage was 25 cents an hour. By 1995 it had risen to $4.25 an hour (it was $3.35 for most of the 1980s), but it was worth less in purchasing power than my dollar an hour at age 16. It was raised again to $4.75 in 1996 and then to $5.15 in 1998, where it stayed until 2007, reaching its all-time low in purchasing power in 2006 at $4.04 in 1996 dollars. In 2007 the minimum wage rose to $5.85. In 2008 it rose to $6.55, and in 2009 to $7.25. When the minimum wage rises, there is a ripple effect on the whole wage structure as those just above the new minimum also get a bump up in wages to maintain wage differentials between newer and longer-term workers, or less and more skilled jobs.

Nothing generates more controversy among economists than the minimum wage. Some economists look at this issue through the lens of efficiency. Assuming that there are perfectly competitive markets with equal power on both sides of the market, these economists argue that raising the minimum wage will reduce the number of jobs, increase unemployment, and encourage employers to hire "off the books." Wages, they believe, should be based on the value of the worker's product. Since some workers can't produce much value, the minimum wage takes away some of those entry level jobs in which workers can gain some experience and eventually be worth more to employers. Other economists—those who see an economy with imperfect competition, hard-to-measure value added, and unequal distribution of economic power—look at the minimum wage through the lens of equity. These economists believe that a minimum wage sets a reasonable standard for those who are uncertain about just how much to pay or how much to ask for and rewards people for work rather than idleness with an income that puts them, if not above the poverty threshold, at least closer to it. A wage of $7.25 an hour for 2000 hours a year (40 hours a week, 50 weeks) still provides an income of only $14,500 a year.

Do increases in the minimum wage really cause unemployment? Evidence about actual unemployment effects in the economics literature is mixed. The measured effects are generally small. Even if the unemployment rate does rise, at least some of the increase is accounted for by an influx of people into the labor market. Some people who had chosen not to seek work at the old minimum wage, because it didn't pay enough to offset the costs of child care and transportation to work, will, at a higher minimum wage, find work more attractive.

Economists who oppose the minimum wage aren't necessarily hard-hearted. They might argue that we should offer other kinds of assistance to those who work hard but don't earn enough to support themselves and their families. The Earned Income Credit on the income tax has been a major source of poverty reduction among the working poor in the last two decades. So the minimum wage debate raises difficult questions about efficiency and fairness, and about whether markets work well enough on their own or whether they need some occasional guidance and direction.

There is also a widespread belief that minimum wage workers are mainly teens working for spare change while getting some valuable job experience. It's true that teens are most likely to see fewer job opportunities as a result of increases in the minimum wage, but the fact is that most minimum wage workers (about 70%) are adults, many with children.

While economists have been arguing over the minimum wage, social justice activists in the United States have taken the battle one step farther. They argue that the worker is not only worthy of his hire but worthy of being paid enough to rise above poverty. Hence, the living wage campaign. A living wage is higher than the minimum wage of $7.25 an hour. It varies from place to place, mainly reflecting regional differences in the cost of housing. Living wage campaigns have sprung up all over the country, from Maine to California, Michigan to Georgia.

The Atlanta living wage campaign came up with two measures of what the hourly wage would have to be to lift a family out of poverty. One measure used was an annual income at 130 percent of the poverty level, which translated to a living wage of $11 an hour. The other measure was based on a minimum needs budget for a family of three, which came to $13.50 an hour. A local living wage would be lower in rural parts of the nation, higher in urban areas in California or the Northeast.

Typically, living wage campaigns are aimed at local governments. Sometimes a major public employer (like a large university) or even a private employer is the object of a campaign, but local governments are a good place to start, because they are often major employers, and they can extend the living wage requirement to their suppliers, which broadens the reach to parts of the private sector. The first step is to pass an ordinance that ensures the city or county is paying all its workers at least a living wage. The second step is to require contractors with and suppliers to that local government to also agree to pay a living wage. A living wage set by a local or state government will influence wage levels in the area's private and nonprofit sectors as well. Living wage campaigns have been very successful in the nation's larger cities, less so in more rural areas.

So, as you rest from your labors on this Labor Day, consider the plight of those who work long hours at or just above the minimum wage, those whose long hours at often difficult and unrewarding jobs are not enough to get them into decent housing or pay for the essentials of life. As people who benefit from their work, what do we owe them? Market wage? Minimum wage? Living wage? Should we second-guess the market, and if we do, will there be fewer jobs? How do we balance freedom of contract with a commitment to a just wage? There are no easy answers.

- Economics Takes a Holiday -

1ˢᵗ Sunday after Labor Day— Grandparent's Day: Paying for the Golden Years

Grandparents' Day, which falls on the first Sunday after Labor Day, is largely a creation of the greeting card industry. Those of us with living grandparents are urged to honor them by sending greeting cards purchased for the occasion, and those without living grandparents are supposed to honor their memories. Those of us who are grandparents get the best deal of all—cards, visits, maybe even presents. In spite of the commercialism, it's not a bad idea for us to take a moment from our youth-centered culture to think about those who built and maintained the path on which the next generation travels.

The typical media image of a grandparent is someone enjoying the golden years: fishing, playing golf, living in a comfortable retirement village, and enjoying occasional visits from their beloved grandchildren. (Many of these media images are commercials promoting retirement communities or prescription drugs to ease the aches and pains of aging!) A rosy scenario, but one that does not apply to many of those over age 65.

Some senior citizens have no grandchildren (or children), or they don't have a relationship with them. Many of them are still rattling around in the now too-large homes in which they raised their families. Many have lost a spouse—10.1 million senior citizens were living along in 2006, three-fourths of them women. Women are far more likely to outlive their spouses because women tend to marry men older than themselves and also to live longer.

But the biggest illusion in these media images is that senior citizens are generally retired and living comfortably on some combination of pensions, retirement savings, and Social Security while Medicare takes care of their increasing health care costs. The traditional poverty measures, unchanged since the 1960s except for adjusting for inflation, put the poverty rate among the elderly below the average for all age groups—9.7 percent, compared to 12.5 percent for all age groups. But a revised formula developed by the National Academy of Science suggests that poverty in general is higher and poverty among the elderly is actually higher than other age groups. A revised version of the formula makes it less focused on food costs and more reflective of other costs that take up more of budgets for elderly households, such as transportation and health care (after allowing for what is covered by Medicare and Medicaid). This new measure suggests that the poverty rate among those over age 65 is actually 18.6 percent, compared to an overall poverty rate of 15.3 percent. So even with Social Security, Supplementary Security Income, Medicare and/or Medicaid, balancing the budget and maintaining a decent standard of living is a challenge for almost one senior citizen in five. How do they make ends meet?

Many senior citizens continue to work, some full time, others part time. About 15 to 20 percent of senior citizens are still working, compared to 65 to 70 percent for those between 20 and 65 years old. Some older people work because they enjoy their work, but a significant number work because they need the income to make ends meet, and many wonder how they will get by when they are no longer able to work.

Even those households that were classed as middle income before retirement had some nasty surprises in recent years. The drop in the stock market combined with low interest rates on bonds and certificates of deposit meant that projected retirement income from investments fell short of expectations. For those retirees planning to sell their homes and move to smaller houses or relocate to different parts of the country, the housing bust knocked a dent in their retirement plans and the value of their biggest asset.

What about pensions? Only about 37 percent of current retirees expect to receive a pension from their employer, and that percentage is dropping steadily. Many private and some public employers have switched away from the traditional defined benefit pension, funded by employer and employee contributions. The benefits for this type of pension are determined by on the retiree's income while working and the number of years with the firm. Instead, many employers now offer a defined contribution plan, which means that an investment account is created for each employee, to which both the worker and the firm contribute funds. How much the retiree gets depends on the amount contributed and the performance of the investments in that account. With defined contribution plans, the risk (both positive and negative) is shifted from the employer to the retiree.

If work is no longer an option, retirees need some safety net under their income. For most retirees, that safety net is Social Security, which is a combination of insurance and a defined benefit plan. According to surveys, 54 percent of retirees depend on Social Security as a major source of income. It's also frequently the most dependable source. For some, it's the only source.

So what's the best gift we can give our grandparents on

Grandparents' Day? How about making Social Security the safe, dependable source of income they were counting on? That means conservative investment of Social Security funds, adequate Social Security taxes, reasonable decisions about retirement age and the ratio of benefits to earnings, and other modest adjustments that could keep the system going indefinitely. Just because the projected "crisis" in Social Security is still 25 years away doesn't mean that we can postpone addressing this important issue now, not only for our grandparents, but also for ourselves, and our grandchildren. As my grandmother used to say, an ounce of prevention is a whole lot less expensive than a pound of cure.

20ᵀᴴ/21ˢᵀ—The Autumn Equinox: Turning Points and the Business Cycle

The autumn equinox in late September is a holiday that can easily pass us by unnoticed. We are more likely to notice the summer and winter solstices, the longest day/shortest night and shortest day/longest night of the year. But March and September mark the midpoints between those two more dramatic solar dates, when days and nights are exactly equal in length. One equinox is the herald of summer, the other the precursor of winter. In the language of mathematics, the equinoxes are inflection points, or turning points. The direction of the cycle turns. In autumn, the descent into winter that began the day after the summer solstice starts to pick up speed. After the spring equinox, the ascent into summer gains momentum. The change is not that noticeable at the time, but the turning points are real and easily predictable.

To the tribes of hunters and gatherers and herders and farmers from whom we all descend, that seasonal flow of solstices and equinoxes was a loud drumbeat. The rhythm of their days and weeks and months was not guided by watches, clocks, calendars, or day runners. They operated on a celestial clock and a sun-dominated calendar instead of a to-do list. And the loudness of that drumbeat was about survival: bringing the herds in from pasture and grazing land for the winter, slaughtering some to provide food over the winter and to ensure enough food for those that would be kept over, and setting aside the seed corn for spring planting. Their calendars were marked by lambing time, planting time, harvesting time. There was no supermarket to run to in February when the winter stores ran low.

That kind of immediate dependence on the bounty of nature, that chronic threat of hunger and starvation if man and nature jointly did not produce enough to survive the coming winter, anchored our ancestors very firmly to the land and the forces of nature. So these regular, recurring turning points meant much more in an agricultural economy without the benefit of the refrigeration, central heat, and high speed transportation that can keep us warm and well-supplied with fresh fruits and vegetables year round from the other half of the globe.

But if the seasons are less significant to our economy that previously, inflection points have other meanings in modern industrial and post-industrial economies. The cycle of the seasons bears a striking resemblance to the business cycle, and business cycles matter very much to households, firms, and governments. Recessions, like the deep and long one that began in December 2007 and ended in a weak recovery, are marked by job losses, profit declines, and reduced government revenue. Students who graduate from college during a recession have a hard time finding their first job. Retirees living on interest and dividends (along with Social Security) may see their income fall. Governments find more people signing up for food stamps and unemployment benefits, while they have less revenue to fund these programs. It's important to be able to predict these downturns in order to be prepared to deal with them.

The business cycle was largely unknown until the 19th century, when industrialization picked up speed. Suddenly, instead of the cycles of abundance and scarcity, planting and harvest, there were cycles of inventory buildup and drawdown, cycles of new products and firms being introduced and maturing into decline, and cycles of boom and bust in production and sales of consumer durables (appliances, automobiles) and especially in housing. These cycles are much harder to predict than the steady ebb and flow of sunlight. A favorite joke among economists is that forecasting models have correctly predicted nine of the last seven recessions! But business cycles of expansion and contraction, growth and recession, are not random, even if they are not as regular as the coming of the seasons. Inventory cycles generally run around two years, housing cycles about 20 years, and cycles of innovation and maturity of products and firms lie somewhere in between, typically about eight years from recession to recession, peak to peak. Unfortunately, there is some variation in the length of each cycle, so economic forecasters can't anticipate exactly when a downturn will end or an expansion will peak. In the United States, the duration of a recession from peak to trough has been as short as eight months and as long as six years. From 1945 to 2007 there were 11 recessions, with an average duration of 10 months from peak to trough.

In fact, economic forecasters can't even tell that the turning point has occurred at the time. It's at least six to nine months after the start of a recession before statisticians are able to confirm that the nation has, indeed, experienced two successive quarters (six months) of decline in real Gross Domestic Product. That's the official definition of the start of a recession.

Recession watchers anxiously look for signs that what's ahead is not more winter but some inkling of an economic spring—more output, more income, more jobs. Those signs are usually found in the index of leading indicators, a composite number that includes ten measures of economic activity that have historically turned up about six months before the economy begins to recover and turned down about six months before the start of a recession. The ten components of the Leading Economic Index include average weekly hours in manufacturing, initial applications for unemployment insurance, new manufacturing orders (consumer goods and capital goods are entered separately), speed of delivery of merchandise, new residential building permits, the S&P stock index, the inflation adjusted money supply, the spread between long-term and short-term interest rates, and consumer expectations. While these indicators don't have the dependability of the autumn equinox in signaling a certain descent into winter, they can at least help families, firms, and governments do a better job of planning ahead for better (or worse) economic weather.

OCTOBER

12ᵀᴴ—Columbus Day: The First Wave of Immigration

Columbus sailed the ocean blue in 1492, landing on one of the islands of the Bahamas and subsequently other islands in the Caribbean. Americans celebrate the man and the voyage on October 12th, a holiday especially popular with Italians, since Columbus was a native of Genoa. While Non-Native Americans owe Columbus some gratitude, revisionist history reminds us that the encounter was not entirely a positive experience for all concerned. Some groups, in fact, have begun protesting this holiday on behalf of Native Americans.

Columbus's three ships were the first wave of European immigration into, not a vast emptiness, but two continents already heavily populated by non-Europeans. The immigrants brought technology, disease, greed, warfare, and Christianity to the Western Hemisphere, and while they were celebrated in their Spanish homeland, they were not necessarily appreciated by those to whom they brought these dramatic and sometimes devastating changes.

The challenges immigrants created for the natives of the New World are still with us today, in different forms. Modern immigrants do not generally bring technology, disease, warfare, or an unfamiliar religion, but they do bring differences in culture and conflict with the indigenous citizens over jobs and wages, in the United States and elsewhere. Ironically, the most visible and numerous immigrants to the United States are those descended from the invading Spaniards and the natives they encountered, Hispanics from Mexico and Central America.

The culture conflict is real but perhaps less profound than the economic concerns. The movement to make English the official language of the United States and the resentment of children who speak no English when they start school reflect both suspicion of foreigners and resistance to change. But these attitudes compete with the enjoyable discovery of Hispanic arts and music and Mexican restaurants in much of the country and similar discovery and enjoyment of art, music, and food from Asian and African cultures.

The economic effects of immigration are much more complex. There are both costs and benefits associated with immigration, and often the costs fall on one group of existing residents while the benefits accrue to a different group. So there are two important questions. Do the benefits of immigration exceed the costs, or vice versa? And, in either case, who gains and who loses?

If the goal is simply economic growth, immigrants are an

additional productive resource. Most immigrants are young, single males who are willing to do unskilled and semi-skilled work for modest wages. Legal immigrants must be paid at least minimum wage and in turn pay income taxes, social security taxes, sales taxes, excise taxes, and—usually through their landlords—property taxes. If and when their families arrive, they may need more public services such as education, recreation, transportation, etc., but young single males who enter legally contribute more in taxes than they demand in services. Social Security in particular benefits from the influx of younger workers.

For those already here, immigrants may make the economic situation better or worse. If you are an employer, immigrants expand the labor pool and hold down labor costs. If you are a middle to upper income household, it's easier to get household and yard help. But if you are at the bottom of the economic ladder, immigrant workers aren't a benefit; they are competition who keep wages low, take jobs that you might otherwise have had, and compete for a limited supply of affordable housing. The effect of immigration on competition has spread upward as college-educated workers find themselves competing with the graduates of India's excellent technical universities for jobs in the United States. It's true that, when times get hard, many of these immigrant workers go home, cushioning the effect of an economic downturn on low-wage workers, but that's not much comfort.

Of course, if people are prevented from immigrating, some of the jobs may move abroad to where the low wage workers are. The United States has seen this movement of jobs first in textiles and shoes, then in the whole range of more durable and expensive consumer goods from appliances to automobiles to computers.

Cracking down on immigration is no guarantee that your job will not go to someone from another country, either through outsourcing or immigration. The reality is that American workers are competing in a global economy. At least if these workers are in the United States, they are subject to our labor and environmental standards and contributing to the cost of public services.

The global economy, in which Americans compete more intensely than ever with workers from other nations, can trace its roots to Columbus and his voyages of discovery, settlement, and conquest. The gifts he brought to the natives were a mixed bag, and so were the gifts he brought back to Europe: including gold (which caused a great deal of inflation), chocolate, and tobacco. Immigration continues to be a mixed blessing, benefiting some, reducing opportunity and causing losses and dislocation for others. Both trade and migration enable the world to use its scarce resources more efficiently, increasing total output. But unless we as a nation face up to the fact that the mobility of workers (immigration) and capital create some real costs for large segments of society, and try to address those costs, we will continue to have anger, protests, and even violence directed at the immigrants among us.

21ST—ALFRED NOBEL'S BIRTHDAY: THE NOBEL PRIZE IN ECONOMICS

Alfred Nobel was born on October 21, 1833, which is not a holiday that appears on most calendars. He is known for two contributions to the world: the invention of dynamite and the establishment of the Nobel prizes. Instead of celebrating his birthday, his memory is honored in December when the Nobel laureates receive their awards and make their addresses. Upon his death in 1895, his will established the prizes in peace, medicine, physics, chemistry, literature, and, notably, not economics.

The Nobel Prize in economics was not established until 1968, when the Swedish central bank, the Sveriges Riksbank, created an endowment to fund the prize and the administrative expenses. Beginning in 1969, it has been awarded to 67 economists, all but one of them male, 42 of them American, and another five with dual citizenship that includes American. It is considered a very prestigious award. When quoting any one of these 67 in the news, the statement is always preceded by "Nobel Prize-winning economist...."

In general, the award is given for significant original contributions to economic theory. But starting in 1974, when the prize was jointly awarded to Gunnar Myrdal and Friedrich Hayek, there have been political overtones as well. In that year the winners were at opposite ends of the philosophical spectrum in terms of the policy applications of their work. Gunnar Myrdal, who would today be classified as politically liberal or progressive, was very interested in economic development issues and the social and cultural context in which that development took place. Hayek is a favorite among conservative and libertarian economists because of his opposition to central planning and his emphasis on a limited role for government in a market system.

Many prize winners have been recognized for their contributions to traditional economic theory, while other, more controversial choices have affirmed an understanding of economics that focuses on the causes and consequences of market failure of various kinds. The prize, however, has been awarded to economists who lie at many points along the spectrum in their political understanding from libertarian (minimum government, maximum freedom) to liberal (greater equality and access to resources).

An emerging trend in economic thinking in recent decades has been a focus on institutional and behavioral economics. This trend has not gone unnoticed by the Nobel Prize committee. Institutional (or neo-institutional) economics explores the way that historical paths, cultural and political contexts, and the specific "rules of the game" in a particular economy will affect the way in which market forces work and the outcomes of particular policies. Behavioral economics studies the ways in which decisions by actual individuals differ sharply from the role of the rational, self-interested, calculating economic man of traditional theory. In general, behavioral economists conclude that humans as economic actors are motivationally more complicated but cognitively less capable than economic theory assumes. Our motives include the interest of others as well as our own self-interest. But on the thinking side, we just don't think as fast or take as many factors into account as do the computers we develop and use. The thinking processes behind our decisions are not careful complications but are also greatly influenced by habit, intuition, social norms, and the way in which the choices are framed or presented.

It is hard to divide the prize winners into traditional, neo-institutional, or behavioral in their focus because all three elements are usually present in work sufficiently significant and distinguished to earn the Nobel Prize. However, some economists have contributed more heavily to neo-institutional or behavioral understanding of economic processes than others. Among the economists who have been recognized by the Nobel Prize Committee for contributions to economics that are primarily neo-institutional and/or behavioral in nature are Herbert Simon (1978), James Buchanan (1986), Ronald Coase (1991), Gary Becker (1992), Douglass North (1993), John Nash (1994), Amartya Sen (1998), Daniel Kahneman (2002), Thomas Schelling (2005), and Elinor Ostrom and Oliver Williamson (2009). Kahneman and Ostrom are actually not economists by profession and training: Kahneman is a psychologist and Ostrom, the first woman to receive the prize, is a political scientist.

What kind of contributions did these eleven winners make? Each of them was concerned with context and/or behavior. They cannot be classified neatly into liberal or conservative, libertarian or progressive. Simon gave us the term bounded rationality, which means that we make our decisions within a limited set of options. Buchanan stressed the importance of the constitutional rules in protecting us from having those with political power use it to further their own self-interest. Coase is famous for showing how conflicts of property rights can be resolved privately if the number of parties is small enough and transactions costs are not too large. Gary Becker expanded economic theory to take on such issues as motivations to marry and have children or commit crimes. North is an economic historian who gave economists a favorite phrase, "path-dependent state," which freely translates as "you are where you are because you've been where you've been, and that limits the options for where you go from here." Nash, made famous by the movie *A Beautiful Mind*, helped us to understand some of the strategic elements of economic decisions. Amartya Sen focused on issues of inequality and the context of rules and processes that can lead or has led to poverty, famine, and other social ills. Kahneman helped to explain some of the mental processes such as framing and attitudes toward risk that would lead people to make choices that do not jibe with the rational, self-interested model of human behavior. Schelling's work focused on the collective consequences of individual choice. He pointed out that our failure to co-ordinate decisions may result in less satisfactory outcomes than we would have chosen in everything from housing segregation to seating at concerts to investment and unemployment. Ostrom's contributions are in the area of management of common pool resources, which do not fit neatly into traditional models. Oliver Williamson's contribution helped us to understand the role of transactions costs in influencing economic decisions.

 The work of these Noble Prize-winning economists and others like them has resulted in a less tidy and mathematical understanding of economic process, but it has also provided a firmer foundation for making economic policy that reflects how actual people think and how the existing social rules (laws, customs, social norms) affect the outcomes of economic policy. Twenty-first century economics is much richer and more useful as a guide to policy as a result of the emergence of neo-institutional and behavioral economics. So it was very appropriate for so many of the Nobel prizes in economics to be awarded to these creative souls who expanded the horizons of traditional economics and explored how economic theory works with real people in particular contexts, which is so important for making good policy.

31st—Halloween: Taking Chances

Halloween is an unusual holiday, a blend of pagan and Christian customs. The ancient Celtic holiday of Samhain was celebrated on November 1st, when the wall between this world and the next was thinnest and spirits walked the earth. Samhain marked the start of winter in northern Europe. The last of the fields were harvested and the animals were brought in for either shelter or slaughter as the cold and dark season approached. Its Christian incarnation is as All Saints' Day or All Hallows' Day, when Christians remember those who have died in the faith. The night before, All Hallows' Eve or Halloween, is still celebrated with an assortment of pagan customs, while the day itself is generally a major religious holiday for Catholics and many Protestants as well. (Hispanics and others also celebrate November 2nd, All Souls' Day, as the Day of the Dead.)

The pagan customs that still persist on Halloween include trick or treat, ghosts and goblins, dressing up in costumes, and bobbing for apples. Among the haunts on your doorstep on Halloweens past have been such scary faces as Richard Nixon, Darth Vader, and Osama bin Laden, along with superheroes like Spiderman, Harry Potter, and Batman. But they share the stage with the standard and more traditional repertoire of ghosts, skeletons, vampires, devils, and witches. However you may celebrate, this holiday is a chance to let your fears, your ghosts and goblins, all hang out—and face up to them.

If you don't have bugaboos of your own to flaunt on Halloween, recent economic problems have generated more than enough ghosts and vampires to meet the needs of the season. There are the ghosts of manufacturing jobs lost, of 401-Ks gone to the great hereafter, of scary banks, upside-down mortgages, and double digit unemployment rates. For those looking for more exotic threats, there is global warming, species extinction, and the prospect of Yellowstone as a supervolcano swallowing up most of the United States. Will all those actual and potential dirty tricks, where are the treats? Amidst all this horse manure, where is the pony?

So far there is no pony, but there is a lesson to be learned that may lead us to wiser and more cautious choices in the next decade. The important lesson of this first decade of the 21st century is about risk. It's about knowing what the risk is in investing in derivatives, real estate, or the stock market and not believing everything the salesperson tells you. It's about the riskiness of depending on your employer for your health insurance and your retirement pension. It's about the limits to how much risk we can shift to the government in demanding that it provide deposit insurance, pension guarantees, health insurance, unemployment compensation, disaster relief, bail out for big firms like banks and auto producers, and prevention of terrorist attacks. It's also about how we pay the bill for all that risk-shifting when it comes due, because we as a nation seem to be violently opposed to the kind of higher taxes other countries pay to have a public safety net.

When the government underwrites risk, it protects us from the consequences of our own negligence, carelessness, and ignorance. So we take greater risks than we would if we had to face the consequences ourselves. If the government will back your firm up when it fails or bail you out when you take financial or health risks, you might take chances that you wouldn't if it weren't for the safety net of your rich Uncle Sam. Insurers call this problem moral hazard. If you have insurance, you are likely to be more careless than if you don't. If you have Social Security guaranteed by the government, you will probably save less for your own retirement. If your bank deposits are insured, you look for the highest rate of return rather than the safest bank.

There is some optimal level of government guarantee against risk. In the past, it has been accompanied by regulations to ensure that people don't take too many risks. Federally subsidized flood insurance is not available in some high risk areas where people might otherwise build and be flooded away multiple times, at high cost to the rest of us. Until three decades ago, banks were strictly regulated to limit their risk exposure by regulating their reserve obligations, their capital ratios, and the kinds of instruments in which they could invest. Alan Greenspan, the former Fed chair and longtime advocate of free financial markets, was heard several years ago publicly admitting that while he had once believed that financial markets could be self-regulating, he no longer believed that it was the case.

Much of the progress we have experienced as a nation has been the result of risk-takers, from the Pilgrims and pioneers to the inventors and entrepreneurs. But risk has a downside. For every success there are multiple failures. If we insure against failures, we create a demand for failure, and there are plenty of individuals and firms willing to supply to that demand. So choose your risks, your goblins, and demons, with care. Your fellow taxpayers will be grateful for the treat.

NOVEMBER

11ᵀᴴ—VETERANS' DAY: PAYING WHAT WE OWE

November 11th is Veterans' Day, when we honor those who fought in America's wars. Every year, there are fewer and fewer living World War II vets, but there are still plenty of veterans from the Korean, Vietnam, Gulf, Iraq, and Afghanistan wars who deserve our respect and appreciation. This holiday began in 1919 as Armistice Day to commemorate those who served in World War I, which ended on November 11, 1918, at the eleventh hour of the eleventh day of the eleventh month. In 1954, it was changed to Veterans' Day to honor all veterans. According to the Census, in 2010 the United States had about 22 million veterans, including about nine million who were 65 or older.

Our military, especially the enlisted men and women, are not very well paid, particularly considering the risks they take, the frequent moves and family separations, and the difficult working conditions for those in combat areas. Pay for enlisted members of the military ranges from about $15,000 a year for a raw recruit to more than $60,000 for the highest ranking members with 20 years of service. They also receive a subsistence allowance to pay for meals and health care.

A substantial part of military compensation is deferred, or paid after active service. Men and women who enlist in the military are made aware at the time of enlistment that these deferred benefits are part of their compensation. Like their civilian counterparts, active duty military can look forward to retirement pensions, but they also can count on continued health care and commissary and PX privileges. They also have access to other benefits that are much less common for civilian workers, including education assistance for themselves and their dependents, home loans, survivor benefits, life insurance, and vocational rehabilitation. Education assistance, home loans, and vocational rehabilitation are not needed by everyone who leaves the military, but they are available to those who need or want these services.

These benefit programs are administered through the Department of Veterans' Affairs, which became a cabinet department in 1989 and currently has a budget of about $60 billion. One of its major functions is to manage the VA health care system, which includes 171 medical centers, more than 350 outpatient, community, and outreach clinics, and 126 nursing home care units.

Deferred compensation and benefits are commonplace in both the public and private sectors. In the public sector, one important plus for using deferred benefits for the military is spreading the cost of war over both wartime and peacetime budgets instead of having budgetary "spikes" in the war years.

In the private sector, the most common form of deferred compensation is a pension, perhaps with retiree health benefits. In recent years, some private employers have reneged on those promised benefits, either by changing the retirement program or by failing to adequately fund it. The federal government has attempted to protect workers at private firms through the Pension Benefit Guarantee Corporation. It is funded by insurance premiums paid by firms with defined benefit pension plans, the assets of the pension plan when it is taken over, and investment income. But those resources have proved inadequate, so the ultimate guarantor is the taxpayer. At least the military have a somewhat more secure commitment from the federal government, although even they have experienced some unexpected and unwelcome changes in benefits from time to time.

Why are deferred benefits so much more heavily used in the military than in civilian careers? A career in the military is likely to be shorter (and perhaps more intense) than a civilian career, whether in the public or private sector. Combat duty or combat support is physically demanding and usually suited to younger people. Constant relocation takes its toll on military families. Expecting a shorter time span of fitness (and willingness) for active duty from most recruits, military pensions are made attractive after 20 years of service, when the retiree is likely to still be young enough to start a second career. Some of the other deferred benefits, like home loans and/or tuition for education, are designed to make that transition smoother.

There are also many retirees or disabled veterans who leave the military with some kind of chronic or recurring medical problem. The military and veterans' health care system is an important kind of insurance for what can be a very high risk occupation. New recruits, even officers, have little idea what kinds of services, benefits, or support they may wind up needing or wanting at the end of their military service.

In the private sector, employee benefits programs grew rather haphazardly largely in response to tax incentives. Most fringe benefits are not subject to income taxes, while wages and salaries are. Congress has been reconsidering that tax status now as the nation works its way through the maze of health insurance reform, because employer-provided health insurance is one of the most expensive fringe benefits. But except for retiree health benefits and pensions, most private sector fringe benefits are part of current rather than deferred compensation. There is no system of nursing homes for retired auto workers, no education benefits or subsidized home loans for those ending their careers in insurance or data processing.

Military service is a unique occupation—not a career to last a full working lifetime for most people, subject to high risk both physically and psychologically, with relatively low pay and frequent moving around that disrupts family life and spouses' careers. A healthy and diverse package of deferred benefits is one of the ways we say thank you to those who have undergone those traumas and challenges on behalf of a grateful nation.

- November -

4ᵀᴴ Thursday—Thanksgiving: Affirming Our Values

Thanksgiving is a blend of religious and secular customs that is celebrated at different times in different places. It's a harvest festival, a celebration of the bounty of nature, and since harvest seasons vary by latitude, there is no perfect date. In the United States, the late November holiday is well past harvest in the north, right at the last of the garden bounty in much of the south, and during the perpetual harvest of a few far southern states. That's probably why Canada celebrates Thanksgiving six weeks earlier!

As we turn from the season of peaches, blueberries and watermelon to the season of apples, winter squash, and collards, we gather not only the food but also the family to huddle together against the coming darkness, cold, naked trees, and dormant gardens. For one day we eat a sumptuous meal, watch parades and football games on television, maybe rake the last of the fall leaves, and then turn our attention to the second phase of the two-day holiday, Christmas shopping. But first, let's look at the day itself, and the attitudes and emotions that underlie a thanksgiving celebration, attitudes like thankfulness, gratitude, and acknowledging our interconnectedness with others.

Economics is not very focused on attitudes, emotions, and values, all of which are embraced by the idea of giving thanks. Economic man (or woman) is rational, self-interested, and calculating. All of us are like that in some aspects of our lives, but economics does not take into account the influence of the rest of what we are—thinking, yes, but also feeling, caring, giving. Those parts of our brain are what Adam Smith, the father of modern economics, called moral sentiments. His classic work *The Wealth of Nations* was preceded by his equally significant but less known work, *The Theory of Moral Sentiments*. Adam Smith was a moral philosopher. His explanations of the self-managed workings of the market were premised on a broader view of human motivation than just the rational, self-interested, calculating part.

Economics is a subset of moral philosophy, and while it seems to have moved away from its origins, many contemporary economists are moving back. Behavioral economics is the latest wave in a series of challenges to the simplistic model of how humans think and behave. It draws on psychology and learning theory to try to comprehend how actual people behave when confronted with new choices, new circumstances, or new challenges or opportunities in the marketplace. Economics as a discipline is slowly changing under the influence of this new understanding. So is public policy.

What kinds of insights do we get from behavioral economics? One example is the behavioral economist's challenge to the economic prediction that people will not cooperate unless it is in their self-interest to do so. Experiments from psychology identify circumstances under which cooperation or collaboration is likely, even if it flies in the face of self-interest. Repeated interaction with the same person or small group makes cooperative and sometimes even altruistic behavior more likely. Most of us already had an intuitive sense of that behavior from noticing the difference in how people interact in small towns versus large cities. Other insights from psychology help us understand the nature of asset bubbles (the dot.coms, the housing market, financial assets), as a bandwagon mentality overcomes the inhibitions of rational calculation. Framing—the way an issue is presented and the images and catch phrases associated with it—will often lead people to vote for candidates or support programs that are contrary to their economic self-interest. Attitudes toward risk are far from rational. Short-term wishful thinking often leads us to costly errors in providing for our own future. We behave differently when confronted with an opt-out situation (we rarely opt out) than when it is an opt-in situation, even though the options we are considering are exactly the same. If we have to make the effort to make a choice, we are much more likely to just go with the default option.

George Lakoff, the guru of framing issues and identifying values, says that those of us who thought policy was all about presenting the facts and understanding the consequences are sadly mistaken. Facts do matter, but speaking to values, understanding some of the feelings and attitudes of voters and fellow-citizens, customers and suppliers, is the place to start. Once we have spoken to or from the heart, the head will follow. That's a far cry from the rational, self-interested buyer or seller in a competitive market.

So this Thanksgiving, take some time to identify and affirm your core values, including gratitude. As for me, I am going to approach the second day of the holiday by leading with my values. I won't go shopping, because I think shopping should be a more thoughtful, responsible act than is possible in the feeding frenzy of Black Friday. When I do get around to shopping for the holidays, I will take into consideration the option to shop with those I encounter regularly in my little town. I will buy gifts that are environmentally responsible from suppliers that treat their workers, customers, and suppliers fairly. I will not put any of my purchases on a credit card that charges more than 20 percent interest, because, even though I pay off my card every month, some of my fellow card holders can't do that and are accumulating debt for mounting interest they may never escape. I'm taking my values into the marketplace this holiday season. What values are you taking shopping with you?

 # DECEMBER

5ᵀᴴ—National Volunteer Day: Working for Nothing

In the intense concentration of holidays at the end of each year—from Thanksgiving to New Year's Day—it is easy to overlook the somewhat obscure but significant International Volunteer Day. On December 5th, we celebrate volunteers and the work they do for their communities, be it at a local or global level. Volunteer work can be defined as work that has value to other people but is done without expectation of payment.

According to the Corporation for National and Community Service, about 63 million Americans spend eight billion hours in volunteer service each year. The range of volunteer work is enormous, from staffing soup kitchens and helping low-income people with tax returns to building and repairing homes, leading scout troops, coaching youth sports teams, delivering meals to shut-ins, working in hospitals and medical clinics, and advocating for social change. Some volunteer work allows people to use their specialized skills, while other kinds develop skills.

The fundamental economic question is one of motivation. Why do people volunteer, and what can we as a society do to encourage more volunteering? What are the rewards? With a few exceptions, the rewards are not directly monetary, which is the primary motivating force in a market system. One exception is VISTA "volunteers"—a federal program called Volunteers in Service to America. VISTA does actually pay a stipend, which somewhat confuses the notion of volunteering. But the stipend is well below the going wage, so the difference between what participants earn and what they could earn might be considered a volunteer contribution.

Homo economicus—economic man—is motivated primarily by economic rewards. He or she works for pay, changes jobs for higher pay, works harder for more pay. Part of the compensation may be something other than salary—fringe benefits, perks, congenial working environment, or creative freedom—but each kind of compensation can somehow be valued in monetary terms so that one employment package can be compared to another and the most valuable one chosen.

In this world of simple motivation, we have to search for self-interested reasons to volunteer. And there are some. There is work experience which can then be carried forward into the for-pay working environment. For teens, there is something to put on the application form for admission to prestigious colleges and/or scholarships that are based on the applicant's volunteer history. Getting into a better college may well translate into higher earnings down the road. These motives are most likely to appear early in life, in the teens and twenties, but they don't help as much in explaining the volunteer efforts of mature adults.

Another group of volunteers are parents who consider volunteer work an extension of their parenting commitment. Coaching, school programs, scouting, and teaching Sunday school all fall into this category. It's a step away from the purely economic motivation. However, it is an investment in one's children, which in today's society are regarded as a consumption choice. In fact, volunteering in general can be regarded as a consumption choice, as something one does for the inherent satisfaction. This economic explanation would make volunteer work no different from skiing, watching television, going to the theatre, or any of a variety of time-intensive consumption choices. In this view, the benefits to others are incidental; it is the satisfaction and enjoyment derived by the volunteer from the work that is the consumption activity. And unlike some consumption activities, no payment is required!

Digging a little deeper into motivation, however, suggests that the decision to work on a Habitat for Humanity house is a little different from the decision to go skiing in Vail. Some of the satisfaction is derived from exercising one's skills and enjoying the company of fellow volunteers, kind of like attending a party with a hammer or paint brush in hand. But some of the satisfaction comes from experiencing the pleasure or joy created for the beneficiaries. The advertisements for volunteers (and for contributions) emphasize that aspect of volunteering. The happiness of others, the motive of altruism rather than self-interest, or the blending of those two motives, has always been troubling for economists to deal with.

Sociologists can help us sort out the motives for volunteering. While economic man is in relentless pursuit of self-interest, sociological man is guided by social norms and expectations. His or her motivation is to be part of a community, to be accepted, to have meaningful interactions with others, to be a part of an environment that allows people to flourish and live meaningful, satisfying lives. To be accepted, respected, and valued in the community requires that one show concern for others. Doing volunteer work is one way to become socially accepted.

The relatively new field of behavioral economics looks at the motives behind our choices—including the choice to volunteer—as more complicated than just simple self-interest. We are driven by both self-interest and altruism. We are both individuals and members of society or communities. We want to be economically secure; we want to enjoy the material pleasures of life. But we also want to be loved, admired, and accepted, and we care about the experiences of others, especially those close to us—family, friends, neighbors, co-workers, and people in the same city or town. As British author E.B. White once remarked, "When I get up I the morning I can't decide whether to enjoy the world or improve the world. It makes it hard to plan my day."

Some kinds of consumption are enhanced by sharing. That ski trip is more fun with family or friends. A theater experience is enhanced by a large and engaged audience. A college class of 20 is likely to be a richer experience than a class of five (although a class of 100 or more is usually not!) Volunteer work of many kinds offers the same kind of shared experience. In economic terms, volunteerism is simultaneously consumption and production, involving no monetary exchange. The experience and satisfaction is payment enough—a form of barter, in which we give time and skills in exchange for positive experiences. However, volunteer work frequently leads to contributing money as well, as the volunteer appreciates not only the experience but also the enrichment of the community and the lives of its residents that the volunteer organization provides.

A second dimension of behavioral economics is the motivation to work. For economists, work is simple: it is a means to an end, which is earning enough to consume. Earning more means consuming more. But again, the motivation to work is more complex. Work can be a form of self-expression. Work offers intrinsic satisfactions beyond the paycheck. Work gives us social value and brings about encounters with others, because we are social animals. Work makes us feel useful and needed and valued. Perhaps this more complex understanding of why we work explains why so many retired people turn to volunteer work to replace not only the social interactions but also the sense of contribution, of value, and of being part of something larger than themselves that they once gained from paid work.

Albert Einstein once said, "Everything should be made as simple as possible, but not simpler." Reducing our motivations to simple self-interest ignores the complexity and diversity of what makes humans tick. Volunteer work is both an important and useful contribution to society, and it is a persistent challenge to the economist's simplistic view of human motivation.

6ᵀᴴ—Saint Nicholas Day: Is There a Santa Claus?

December 6th is the feast day of Saint Nicholas, an ancient bishop of Myra in Asia Minor long since transformed into the jolly old elf of *Twas the Night Before Christmas*. Saint Nicholas was known for rescuing young virgins from being sold into prostitution by providing them with dowries of gold coins delivered mysteriously in the night. Some of the stories attached to him—the stockings full of treats and the pieces of coal—actually date back to a Celtic goddess of the underworld, Mother Holle, who rewarded the good and punished the bad at this time of year. But Mother Holle has long disappeared from the scene, perhaps morphing into the obscure Mrs. Claus who lives at the North Pole and manages a household full of worker elves.

The Santa Claus story is problematic for parents. Should they encourage their children to think there is a mysterious gift giver who flies in a reindeer-driven sleigh around the world in one night delivering gifts to all good children? How do they explain the Hispanic neighbors who share their religious tradition but whose children get their gifts on January 6th from the three kings? Or children whose religious traditions don't involve Christmas at all—Muslims, Hindus, Buddhists, Jews, or people of no particular faith? At what point do we admit that Santa is a charming myth, a symbol, a metaphor for the spirit of love and generosity and good will that we celebrate at this time of year?

Santa Clause is problematic for economists as well, because

a Santa figure is one who gives limitless gifts with no apparent resources (except elves) to produce them and expects nothing in return. No market exchange going on there! Objects—toys, puzzles, candy, and the like—are materializing out of thin air. It goes against the grain of that most fundamental of economic beliefs, namely that there is no such thing as a free lunch. Economists said that so often that Milton Friedman reduced it to an acronym, TINSTAAFL, thereby saving economists precious time in saying all nine words. Everything has an opportunity cost, and the sooner we learn that, the better. If we want a bike, we have to realize that it means we can't have a new Wii game or a skateboard. We have to order our priorities, make our choices, and recognize that more of one thing means less of something else.

At one level, the economists are right. The Santa Claus myth does encourage some disengagement with reality. Scarcity and choice is the meat and potatoes of economics, and Santa Claus is about abundance, not scarcity. The prevalence of this faith in Santa's unlimited resources is particularly hard on low-income parents. They have to explain why the wealthier children in their school were treated so much better by Santa Claus, why some child received not only a bike but also a skateboard and a Wii game while the poor child got just a few simple inexpensive toys. Opportunity cost only seems to matter in some households. Furthermore, some of those Grinch-like economists might argue, children who grow up believing in Santa Claus are likely to transfer that faith in generosity and unlimited resources to government and expect the government to provide for their needs and wants without expecting anything in return—like taxes willingly and ungrudgingly paid. And parents who teach their children about an illusion only to have to disillusion them at a later date are undermining their own credibility. Perhaps we should ground our children in reality, and the sooner, the better.

Santa Claus does indeed stand in tension with the plodding reality of scarce resources and tradeoffs and calculations and priorities, but perhaps that is precisely why he is so important to children. Economist Kenneth Boulding once drew a sharp contrast between economic man—calculating, pedestrian, narrowly focused—and heroic man—visionary, hopeful, altruistic. Ebenezer Scrooge in Dickens *A Christmas Carol* was a paradigm of economic man before his epiphany. Santa Claus is closer to heroic man, embodying kindness, generosity, and limitless possibilities. He exists outside, above, and beyond the narrow fixations of the bean-counters and profit-seekers of the market, which embodies impersonal relationships, self-interested behavior, and scarcity.

Children need both. So do adults. Some grounding in reality, and some flights of a hopeful imagination. We need both roots and wings, roots to anchor us, wings to let us soar. At this time of year, when the days are short and cold and we huddle together waiting for the warmth and light to return, perhaps we all need, for just a few weeks of the year, a touch of Santa Claus in our lives.

- December -

Late December—Winter Solstice/Christmas/ Hanukkah: Throwing Hope into the Darkness

Somewhere around the 21st of December, the Northern Hemisphere experiences its shortest day and longest night of the year. This winter solstice officially marks the start of winter. After that date, even though the coldest part of winter is yet to come, the gradually lengthening days inspire hope in all of us who yearn for spring.

There is a historical cluster of religious holidays associated with this event. The ancient Romans celebrated the Saturnalia at this time of year, and even though the date of Jesus's birth is unknown (probably October), the church chose to blend the celebration of his birth in with the general festivities of the season. In part, the symbolism of hope and renewal at the darkest time of year was an appropriate and meaningful link between the Christian faith and the turning of the year. Hindus celebrate Diwali, a festival of lights. Jews observe Hanukkah, another festival of lights, which commemorates the rebuilding of the temple. Pagans celebrate the solstice as the earth mother once again giving birth to the sun. The common theme here is a cycle of rebirth, renewal, and hope.

The dance of earth and sun is not the only kind of cycle humans encounter. There are cycles in the history of nations, cycles of growth and decay in the life of plants and animals, and, for economists, cycles in economic activity. Recovery from a recession in many ways parallels the solstice, because it involves renewal and the rebirth of hope. A hint of recovery finds us looking anxiously for signs of new life just as we search our yards for emerging daffodils and crocuses. Public officials seize on good news—profits, employment, sales—to encourage households to spend and business firms to hire, trying to give hope a boost.

While the earth sends forth clear signals of renewal, the economy is a little harder to gauge, because there are multiply measures, which sometimes point in different directions. For economists, the official measure of recovery is increases in the Gross Domestic Product, or total output. While you would expect we would measure output by adding up production, in fact we measure it by the purchasers—consumption by households, investment by business firms, government purchases, and net exports sold to other countries. The reason for adding it that way is that it is demand by buyers that drives production. No firm is going to produce anything that isn't likely to find buyers.

By far the largest component of GDP is consumption, or purchases by households of services and tangible goods. Consumers are more likely to spend if they are optimistic about their own financial future, if, in other words, they have a job (or two), some money in the bank, and not too much debt. They also look at their assets—savings, pension funds, and the value of the equity in their home. If all those numbers look positive, they will start spending again. If not, they will build up their savings, pay down their debt, and postpone or slow down the recovery from a recession. So one of the most interesting numbers that economists watch is the index of consumer expectations. As we are learning, consumers are not the simple, rational, calculating machines of traditional economic models. They are a complex mix of hope and fear, self-interest and altruism, caution and foolhardiness. They often exhibit herd instincts and pick up cues for their economic expectations and behavior from their friends and neighbors and from the media.

There are two indexes that measure consumer expectations. One is the Conference Board Consumer Confidence Index, published monthly, which surveys 5,000 households about their expectations for their personal income and employment, as well as general conditions like inflation and interest rates. The other index, also based on surveys, is the index of consumer sentiment produced by the University of Michigan. That index is one of ten components of the index of leading indicators, which is used to forecast economic conditions six to twelve months ahead. The other components include changes in inventories, housing starts or building permits, new unemployment claims, interest rates, and the money supply.

How do consumers arrive at their expectations? It's a blend of personal experience and news information. If the government and the media lean heavily on the good news and downplay any bad news, they can encourage consumers to think more positively and go out and spend. But if the good news on television doesn't mesh with personal experience, consumers are likely to go with their gut—and their bank balance.

It's possible to hurry an economy along, but it won't go far or fast on persuasion alone. Generally governments will supplement the "good news" approach with some kind of active stimulus to actually increase jobs and bank balances. Republicans tend to prefer tax cuts and Democrats spending programs, but they generally agree that sometimes a push from government can help to speed the recovery process. Ultimately the expansion has to become self-sustaining, and that depends on the willingness and ability of consumers to spend. Government may have the power to tax, and businesses, the power to create jobs, but only consumers have the power to determine how fast the economy is going to grow—or not. So a renewal of hope is critical, whether it is needed to get us through a cold and dark winter or a cold and dark economic downturn.

- December -

26ᵀᴴ—Boxing Day: Opening the Box

December 26th, the day after Christmas, is Boxing Day in the United Kingdom, Canada, New Zealand, and Australia. Somehow the United States got left out of the family of former British colonies in this instance. Boxing Day isn't part of our holiday tradition, although perhaps it should be.

The box of Boxing Day is not the empty gift box that held a shirt or a necklace or a video game. It's a particular kind of box. A Christmas box was once a clay box used in artisan shops. Apprentices, masters, visitors, and customers would put money into it all year. The day after Christmas, it would be shattered and shared among the workers. A combination tip jar and Christmas bonus, its origins extend back to feudal times when the lord of the manor was expected, indeed obligated, to give boxes of practical gifts such as cloth, grain, and tools to his serfs at this time. The church's poor box was also opened on Christmas Day, and the contents were distributed to the poor the next day.

So this somewhat obscure holiday is not about the sport of boxing, or about boxing up the gifts you don't want and either returning them to the store or inflicting them on the needy. Boxing Day is about sharing, and more than that, it's about the obligation to share with those who are less fortunate. Sharing is a year round obligation, but from our agricultural past we are aware that the needs are greatest at this time of year when the earth is taking a sabbatical from food production in the northern hemisphere and the cold and dark requires more fuel and clothing for warmth and light. For the serfs on the manor, the Boxing Day distribution was not charity; it was their right and due as participants in the manorial economy. For the workers in the Victorian shops, it was part of their earned compensation, a tidy lump sum after 52 weeks of just getting by on barely adequate wages. These customs live on in certain parts of the market economy in Christmas bonuses, profit-sharing, and the occasional worker-owned cooperative or employee stock ownership plan. But for the most part, the end-of-year distribution has been moved from the center of the economy to the fringes with surges of holiday generosity to charities who serve the poor.

Joseph Singer, a Harvard Law professor and a Talmudic scholar, writes in *The Edges of the Field* that (according to Hebrew scripture) those who own land are obligated to share the fruits of the land with those who are landless. We must not harvest up to the edges of the field, but leave something for the gleaners to take to sustain themselves. That practice is not charity, but an interpretation of the meaning of property law and property rights in a nation that was bound together by covenant. The central point of Joseph Singer's book, and of some other writers on the subject of property rights in recent years, is that every right implies an obligation or a responsibility. Not charity, not largesse, not upper class benevolence to the lower classes, but duty, responsibility, obligation. If I have a right to an education, citizens have an obligation to provide it. If you have a right to be safe in your home from thieves and intruders, the rest of us have an obligation to fund a police force for your protection, while you yourself have an obligation to take reasonable precautions like locking your doors.

In *The Theory of Moral Sentiments*, Adam Smith's companion piece to his famous *The Wealth of Nations*, Smith defines a market society as a network of rights and obligations, some personal, some impersonal. *The Theory of Moral Sentiments* provides the ethical framework and motivation to be a good, responsible member of that marvelous, powerful network called a market system. The government's primary role, according to Smith, is to define and enforce some of the rules of the game on which a market system depends, primarily property rights that define the privileges and responsibilities of ownership.

Within that framework, the actions of individuals, based on enlightened self-interest, will lead to the efficient use of resources, thus producing the mix of goods and services people want at prices they are willing to pay, creating jobs and income and opportunities for everyone. Within that framework, we don't need a cumbersome bureaucratic structure to dictate what each serf or artisan or gleaner receives on Boxing Day or during the year in between. But we do need to be mindful that the income and wealth that we enjoy within that system is a product not only of our own efforts but of the work of others, much of it invisible, which has made our success possible. That's where the obligation part comes in, and that's the part that is so easy to forget.

The good outcomes of relying on the market will happen, according to Smith and others, only as long as we do not undermine or weaken the moral seed capital that we have inherited. That inheritance comes from the ancient Hebrew and feudal understanding of society as a covenant of reciprocal obligations and from the medieval craftsmen and artisans who saw the proceeds of Boxing Day as a right rather than a benevolent act of their employers. The Tea Party and other political conservatives are right to call attention to the importance of protecting and defending the rights and privileges we enjoy in a free society, including the right to choose where we live and with whom, to spend our incomes as we see fit, to be safe in our home and possessions, to vote to choose our leaders, to exercise freedom of speech and religion. But political progressives and liberals also remind us that those rights have historically been accompanied by obligations: the obligation to ensure that everyone enjoys the rights of a free society; the obligation to pay taxes; the obligation to pay those who work for us a fair wage, including not just those who work directly for us but those whose earnings we have some say about, like the people who work for our cities or our churches and voluntary organizations; the obligation to help those who have temporarily lost their niche within the system that used to ensure them an income. Boxing Day is a good time to reflect on how we balance our personal and collective books of rights and responsibilities in preparation for the New Year just six days away.

www.ingramcontent.com/pod-product-compliance
Lightning Source LLC
Chambersburg PA
CBHW030008190526
45157CB00014B/1053